Pulitzer or Bust

Trish Tomlins et al.

CHAMPLAIN COLLEGE
Champlain College Publishing

CHAMPLAIN COLLEGE
Champlain College Publishing

This work was supported by Champlain College Publishing. Champlain College Publishing has not undertaken any independent review or assessment of the quality, accuracy, completeness, currentness or other aspects of the content and any views or opinions expressed in this book are the views or opinions of the author(s) and do not necessarily represent those of Champlain College Publishing, Champlain College, or its employees, trustees, or representatives. The author(s) alone are solely responsible for the content of the book and bear all responsibility for any claims arising from the publication of this book.

Second Edition

First printing September 2011

ISBN: 978-0-9834292-2-7

Cover and Interior Design by Aurelia Godard

For information on Champlain College Publishing, see ChamplainCollegePublishing.com

Table of Contents

Introduction

The bookstores are full of Writers-On-Writing books, in which famous authors give advice to writers who are just starting out. Many of these are fine books, and well worth reading, but they tend to assume that the novice writer is a post-college adult.

Anyone who wants to be a really, really good writer has felt the determination and desire to write long before graduating college. He or she has probably been filling up notebooks since the age of 15, or 12, or even 8. By the time college rolls around, especially if the writer-to-be has signed up for a writing program, the advice he or she needs is very different from what would be useful to a novice of 25 or 40.

What's more, the advice he or she needs may not be the advice that a successful author who is, say, 50 years old would give. Some of the wisdom of that established writer may well be worth the price of admission, but some of it may simply not apply to a 19-year-old in an undergraduate writing program.

That student may need to hear from other students a year older, or two years older, or young writers out in the workplace who have recently graduated from a writing program and have a remarkably keen sense of what is really important for someone a year or two behind them.

With that in mind, we offer *Pulitzer or Bust*: a collection of reflections, insights, stories, and pieces of advice from writing students and former writing students, edited and presented by a writing senior on the cusp of graduation.

We've organized it into a year-by-year format because a student's life changes dramatically over six months, let alone 12. Exploration and risk-taking are vital for a young writer, but the risks a first-year student could be taking are very different from the risks involved in that final under-graduate year. Everyone is different, of course, and writers tend to be even more different than people in most other professions, but there's a clear narrative arc to the college experience, and we've tried to respect that.

In the end, all advice to all writers of all ages probably boils down to a combination of four things: read a lot, take your writing seriously, have courage, and take risks. But exactly how to apply those pieces of advice to everyday life—well, let's listen to those who have tried.

Tim Brookes
Director, Professional Writing Program
Champlain College, Burlington, Vermont

Year Zero

You've just graduated from high school, you're planning to head off to college to find out if you have what it takes to be a writer, and someone hands you this book. Why should you read it? In particular, why should you read it now?

You should read it because right now, let's face it, you're feeling a bit pulled in two opposite directions.

On the one hand, you've got all your friends telling you that the summer between high school and college is your last three months of freedom and, come on, you should live your life while you're still young, dude. And they're right.

You've also got your parents hovering over you asking about reading lists and telling you how important it is to prepare yourself for college and avoid the humiliation of flunking out. And they're right, too.

Luckily, it's not an either/or choice. It's a question of thinking about what you can do to help yourself develop as a writer even before you get to college. And it turns out you can do all sorts of things, most of which you'd want to do anyway.

Abby Messick

Don't sit around and do nothing.

Stories don't write themselves. And if you're anything like me, by the time you get around to writing it, you won't even be able to remember what it was you were thinking in the first place.

It's pretty easy to goof off. It's pretty easy to think about writing and never really get around to it. But sometimes all you need to start writing is that one sentence, that one nagging thought that's been hanging around in your head all day. Other days it's harder to start than others, but in the end you'll be thanking yourself. Maybe something you don't like today can turn into something you love. It's good to have a lot of ideas, but it's even better to write them down.

Write over the summer

A writer writes.

That's just a fact. In order to become a successful writer, you have to write.

It's easy to stay in practice while you're in school and you have a teacher breathing down your neck, asking you where your assignments are and constantly reminding you about due dates. It's a lot more difficult to keep up with your writing over the summer when you're working or you have a thousand other things on your to-do list every day. No one cares if you write over the summer. You're the only one who will notice if you stop.

But college isn't like high school—you have a lot more freedom to write what you want to write, when you want to write it. So you have to motivate yourself to keep in the practice of writing, and you might as well start learning right now how to motivate yourself.

The best advice that I can give to you is to write *every single day*.

Evan Litsios

Writing, like any art form, is a beast of routine and discipline. You have infinite opportunities to produce infinite things with your writing, but you won't begin to tap into them unless you begin to devote yourself to the process of creation.

When you're watching TV, you could be reading. When you're playing video games, or chatting on Facebook, or spacing out thinking about random things on your stoop, you could, and should be writing.

Write every day. If you are into routine and schedule, schedule time. If not, just promise yourself that you'll write at some point, for more than 40 minutes, before the day is over. You will see positive change in your writing after just five days, I promise, but like anything it may come in a package that you don't expect.

With all that said, I also want to stress the importance of patience, because you won't be a good writer tomorrow or the day after. It takes time. So lower your head and slam it against the writing desk every day, and eventually, your brains might spill out onto the page in a bloody heap. That day, you'll at least be something, which is all that I can really guarantee.

You don't need to write a Pulitzer Prize-winning piece every single day. You don't even need to write anything that you like or will use again. Just the act of writing every day will help you to become a better writer. Writing is a skill that may come naturally to you, but you won't improve at all unless you work to improve. The goal should always be to become the best writer that you can possibly be, and keeping in practice writing will only aid you in that goal.

This doesn't mean you need to be writing formal, finished, complete pieces every day. Keep a notebook beside your bed so if a thought pops into your head into the middle of the night, you can jot it down before you go back to sleep and forget. Keep a diary logging your day's events—it's therapeutic to reflect on yourself, and it's an effective way to track your progress as a writer. (It also helps you get used to the sound of your own writing voice.)

Carry a scrap piece of paper in your pocket so you can jot down thoughts as you're walking down the road. Draft messages in your phone of everything on your mind. Make a list of your interests. Create a bucket list. Write stories. Write poetry. Write essays. Write lists of weird things people say or wear. Write lists of great potential names for bands or titles for albums. Just write about something you're passionate about. Soon you'll see how easy it is to keep in practice every day and how much fun you have doing it.

This brings up a very important side-point: in high school, you spend an awful lot of time writing things you're not passionate about, and that kind of pretentious, empty, dull writing can become a habit. A bad, bad

> Just write about something you're
> passionate about. Soon you'll see
> how easy it is to keep in practice
> every day and how much fun you
> have doing it.

habit. You can even get to the point where you don't know what to write about unless someone tells you, and you are a slave to the writing prompt. Make that one of your summer goals: discover what it is you actually want to write about.

Emily Murnane

Don't ever be afraid to write something awful. Sometimes the bad writing turns into beautiful writing; sometimes it just stays bad. All I know is that I've never written a masterpiece in a single draft. In fact, some of my best writing started out as embarrassing, painful-to-read first drafts.

The thing about writing is that theory alone won't make you any better. You just have to do it yourself. The more you write, the better you get–even if you don't think much of the writing is very good. If you're really that pained by it, you don't have to show it to anybody. Just make sure that you write it, first of all, and that you don't throw it away. Keep your bad writing for two reasons. One, so you can see what mistakes you made and make sure you don't keep making them. Two, so you can rewrite, if you want, and turn it into something great.

I used to be scared, sometimes, to put things down on the page because I knew they weren't going to turn out the way I wanted. Now that I'm starting to accept that fact, I'm writing more than ever and coming out with more and more pride-worthy pieces.

Make a list of your interests

Everyone is interested in something. What makes people unique are their interests and the things that they use those interests to accomplish. What makes you unique as a writer is that you have different interests than all of the other writers around you, and because of that, you have different things to write about and share with an audience.

As a writer, it's your job to be interesting, and the first step toward being interesting is to be interested, to find things that interest you.

College is the time to explore your interests. Even before you get to college, then, take the time to think about the things that intrigue you and the things that you think you may want to write about. Even if you're on the fence about something, what's the harm in exploring it to make sure it's not something that you secretly love? You'll be surprised what strikes your fancy and what you get the most out of writing about. Even if it seems silly or like it will lead you nowhere, there isn't any harm in considering it as an option.

Write down the things that interest you that you think you may want to explore during your four years at school, whether in class or outside of class. Write down outlandish things. Write down things that in a million years you don't think a class will be offered on.

Then go onto your chosen school's website and flip through all the classes that they offer. See if anything else pops out to you. See if there's a class completely unrelated to the writing curriculum that you simply have to take, just because it sounds so interesting. There's writing in everything, and it's your job to find your niche and make your interests work for your major.

Kayleigh Blanchette

Over the summer, I made a list of everything that interests me in order to help me define the area of writing I want to make a career of. I listed: film, black American history, food, alternative health, women's rights, animals, 1960s studies, performance arts, improv comedy, life stories, cults, and interior design. I could combine any of these with writing, and voila, I have a job.

Broaden your reading

Yes, you might prefer to spend the entire summer hanging out by the pool or stuck in the darkness of your room playing *Final Massacre VIII*. But the fact is, you have a potentially lively mind that right now is as receptive as a sponge, and apart from learning a few new yells and grunts, playing *Final Massacre VIII* is going to do nothing for you as a writer. Even if you're planning to be a game writer, you should assume that the storylines you will write and the characters you will invent as a professional game writer will be a darn sight more interesting than anything that is on the market right now.

Start reading like a fiend. Once college starts, you'll be dismayed at how little time you have to read. Take advantage of this long summer break and soak up the words.

Skyler Lendway

Consume as much writing as possible. Books, news-papers, medical journals, billboards, Spanish soap operas—whatever and whoever's writing inspires you to write. In the words of Berthold Hawkeye (a bit character from Fullmetal Alchemist Brotherhood), "If an alchemist ceases to think, he dies."

Well, we writers are in the exact same boat. Never stop writing, never stop thinking, and never stop seeking things that will make you think.

Let's be clear about this. You're not reading to impress people with all the books you've read, or all the great writers you can quote. You're not reading to improve your impressive vocabulary, though that may happen along the way. You're not reading to prove how cool you are because of your vast knowledge of underground writers nobody else has heard of. And you're certainly not reading just to show you've read the books that everyone else has read.

You read to broaden your horizons. That's not to say that if you only ever read graphic novels, now you've got to start reading Shakespeare and the lesser-known German poets of the late 19th century or James Joyce. It's not a matter of genre, or of content. It's a matter of exploring.

You want to see what more experienced writers do with language. You want to see how they play with plot, or with structure. You want to read things that surprise you, because as a writer you're going to want to surprise your reader. You want to bask in colorful, inventive, or funny dialogue, because if you only ever read conventional dialogue you'll only ever think of writing conventional dialogue. You want to spend the summer swimming around in interesting, stimulating writing—because if you don't, how will you ever know what interesting, stimulating writing is? And if you don't know what it is, how will you ever write it?

Christian Belekewicz

Treat the writer in you as if it were your child. Don't be an abusive parent. Hang its goddamn drawings up on the fridge, no matter how messy they may look.

A shopping list

Start reading like a fiend. Once college starts, you'll be dismayed at how little time you have to read.

At no time in your life are your parents more likely to buy you anything you ask for than in the weeks leading up to your first year in college. Take advantage of this weakness.

1. A Moleskine (the final "e" is silent) is a small, hardback notebook ideal for writers. It fits into a pocket, is great for jotting down thoughts, and even has a handy little pocket at the back where you can tuck receipts

or business cards. Don't worry about the strange name: no small furry rodents have been killed to make your Moleskine.

2. **A computer.** A laptop may be slightly more versatile and useful than a desktop, but it's not essential. If you're thinking you may branch into music, e-games, or graphic design, you will probably be better off with an Apple product, but otherwise you could go with either a PC or Mac based on your preference.

3. **A USB flash drive.** Or two. Preferably one that is instantly identifiable as yours, and hard to lose. You'll want this not because you're going to be writing novels so long they require gigabytes of memory, but just so you have somewhere to back everything up. Backing up is going to be so important to you it needs to become a reflex.

4. **A digital audio recorder** may help, especially if you're planning to specialize in journalism and/or oral history. Try to get one with a USB connection that allows you to plug it right into your computer and upload the audio files.

5. **A small digital video camera** is very much part of a writer's trade these days. It allows you to post all kinds of video clips online, whether onto YouTube or your own website or for an online newspaper or for a magazine.

6. **A digital still camera** is very useful. Most phone cameras still don't quite cut it, especially if you're going to be combining words and images in what you create.

Of course, none of these is utterly essential. Writers have historically made do with pens, pencils, the backs of envelopes, even the backs of their hands. These are just conveniences that some of us have found make our lives easier and free up some more writing time.

Q&A with Dan Ritter

Q: Dan, I want to be a better writer. How do you suggest I go about doing that?

A: Read and write a lot.

Q: But I don't have time to read!

A: That's total and absolute bullshit. Make time to read. Make a lot of time to read. It's absurd to think for even a moment that you can get away with even pretending to call yourself a writer if you are not an avid reader. They are two sides of the same coin. If you're not a skilled reader you're not a skilled writer. If you're not carrying a book around with you everywhere you go, I personally think you're fucking up.

Q: How do I make time to read? I'm so busy!

A: Wah, wah, wah. Figure it out, doofus. Read before you sleep. Read on the bus. Read at the start of class. Read instead of signing onto Facebook. Read instead of getting drunk—or, read while drunk. Think about all the ways you waste time in any given day and say to yourself, "Ho-hum, instead of fucking around I could be reading!" If you're not passionate enough about reading to make it a staple of your life, you are probably in the wrong major. You should be as passionate about reading as you are about writing.

Q: So I should read more. What next?

A: Write a lot. See above. You're never going to write a novel unless you actually sit down and start writing—and the writing process is going to kick your ass every step of the way. If you're not willing to stand up after every time you get beat up and fail then you're not willing to be a writer. Writing a poem should hurt. It should be exhausting. If it is easy, you're probably doing it wrong.

Q: Read a lot and write a lot—and writing is hard. Is that it?

A: Not at all. Reading and writing are hugely important, but that's not all there is to this craft. Being a writer means being both an artist and a scientist. As an artist it is your duty to be the creator of meaningful things—it is your duty to make others think, reflect, change, and grow. As a scientist it is your duty to approach your art with rigor, skill, and determination. The scientist in you will develop the tools you need to express yourself. You cannot create things without tools. Become as comfortable with the technical aspects of language and storytelling as you are lying in bed with a loved one. The better you are with your tools, the better you will be at creating things.

Q: Sometimes I have a hard time coming up with things to write about—writer's block, you know?

A: If you honestly don't think you have anything to write about—if you think your brain is so empty and boring that you have nothing interesting to put on the page—then for God's sake go out and do something interesting. Go for a walk, sit in a tree, kiss a pretty girl, get arrested, whatever. Writer's block is just an excuse to become a more interesting person.

Dan's advice may sound like tough love, or perhaps even brutal love, but he raises a vital question you may not have thought about quite enough: are you sure you want to be in a writing program? From a distance—in other words, from high school—writing at college may seem like a fun option, or even an easy option, but it's not. As a writer, everything you do for the rest of your life will require your inspiration, your energy, and your initiative to make it happen. Words don't appear on the page by themselves. Writing can be the most exciting and fulfilling career, not only a profession but a calling—but it's not for the lazy, and it's not for those who wait around for someone to tell them what to do next.

Oh, yeah—one last thing. Just in case the writers we quote sound as if they know it all and have it all together, remember that the only reason they're giving that particular piece of advice, the reason why it means so much to them, is because they learned it the hard way: by screwing up. We're all human around here. We're all learning. Come and join us.

First Year

Your first year in college is the most stressful planned event in your life. Death in the family, divorce, loss of job—all of these are devastating, but that's in part because they're unplanned and often unexpected. College— well, you've actually chosen to be here. Nobody to blame but yourself!

Even though college is a sheltered environment compared with the real world in which you'll have to make a living, a great deal about it is new, and you may not know how to deal with it. The roommate who insists on shutting the window and cranking the heat, insisting she has a medical condition and can't sleep if it's less than 85 degrees? The guys down the hall who are trying to make it into the *Guinness Book of World Records* by playing a 300-hour beer pong marathon? The cafeteria food, which seems to consist of nothing but nine foods you're allergic to, plus unseasoned tofu?

It would be tempting to retreat to your room, wrap yourself and your laptop in your comforter and do nothing but watch *Buffy* reruns or play *World of Warcraft*. But you are a writer, and if you retreat from the world, after a while your short, bitter poems about dorm life or your endless novel of zombie warfare will get a bit stale. A writer needs input—and the first year of your college life, if nothing else, will be full of potential input. So the trick is going to be to say loudly to yourself, "I thrive on chaos!" and head out into the existential mayhem all around you, notebook in hand, to make the most of it.

Haley Kenyon

Let's face it. Writing isn't as easy as we all made it out to be before college. In high school, it was for fun. I thought I was amazing, and that I didn't need classes. I was terribly, terribly wrong.

Day One

When you first arrive at college, and especially when you sit down in your first writing class, you're likely to feel intimidated.

Maybe it's the dark, silent, brooding students who intimidate you because they seem so intense and, well, deep. Perhaps it's the talkative ones who seem to have an answer to every question and all the confidence in the world, or at least in the room. It could even be the ones who don't say or do anything at all, but you're convinced that they're all silently judging you. And then there are the ones who let on that they've already finished their first novel, or that their uncle is head of new program development at NBC.

Then again, perhaps it's the teacher who intimidates you. There's a pretty good chance that he or she will start out asking you questions that are different from anything any teacher asked you in high school, questions you've never thought about and you're not even sure how to think about. There's a very good chance that he or she will ask you to do writing activities that are new to you, and will then invite the whole class to discuss what you've written.

Or maybe—and this is very likely indeed—it's the whole subject of writing that has suddenly become intimidating. Until now, writing has meant a poetry class with a teacher you liked and really brought it all alive, or a stint on the school newspaper or literary magazine. Now it seems so serious, even threatening.

Okay, let's stop and step back for a minute.

First of all, let's think about the other students who seem intimidating.

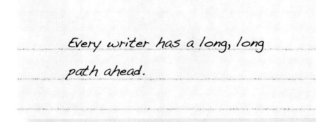

Every writer has a long, long path ahead.

Fact is, you don't know anything about them yet, so that intimidation is all of your own making. The silent ones may be silent not because they're deep, but because they're scared to say anything. The talkative ones may be anxious and eager for other people's approval. Everyone is judging everyone else, for sure, but everyone is judging themselves far more harshly. The whole situation is new and uncertain for everyone, but that novelty will pass, everyone will have survived, and from then on it will be business as usual.

How about the students who already have those great credentials or connections? Are they a sign you're already falling behind?

No. Every writer is different; every writer has a long, long path ahead. It doesn't matter if someone else has already written a novel or published a poem: they're just starting out down that road, same as you are.

Nor does it matter if you don't know what your road is or where you're going. Most writers typically try several different types of writing before hitting the genre that really works for them—and most writers practice several different kinds of writing. A poet will typically also write reviews, and needs to know how to write grant proposals, too. A journalist who can also write more reflective, memoir-style writing has a leg up on other journalists, and might actually get a book contract one day. At this stage, the only mistake you can make is not to try new things.

As for the teacher and the teaching methods, well, yes—college is different from high school and it may take a week or two to adjust, but it won't be impossible. Here's a tip: the very best thing you can do to help that adjustment is to ask questions. Don't be afraid of being a pain in the ass: good teachers like questions. And don't be afraid of sounding stupid: half the class is probably wondering the same thing as you, but they haven't gotten around to asking yet. Asking a good question actually makes you a pathfinder for everyone else.

When it comes to class discussion of your writing, you're going to have to get used to the fact that from now on, you're not just writing for yourself: you're writing for readers, and you need to know what readers like and don't like, what they understand, and what goes over their heads—and the best way to find that out is to hear it from readers who're going through exactly the same journey of exploration and discovery as you.

If the teacher is unkind, unfair or just plain nasty, have a quiet word after class and say s/he's not creating an environment that brings out the best in you. And if that doesn't work, go straight to the dean and complain. You're the one who is paying their salaries, after all, and even though you may have a lot to learn, you deserve to be treated with basic human decency while you're learning.

Haley Kenyon

Stop trying to please everyone else, at least at first. You will never write anything if you expect the first draft to be good. You'll write one sentence, and repeatedly delete it because it's just not perfect. You have to be selfish, you have to say "This one's for me." Second drafts, and third drafts, and hell, 15th drafts are where you start working other people in.

Scout out the landscape

You want to get as much out of your college experience as possible, and that means you don't want to spend your time in your dorm room watching TV.

What's going on around campus, as far as writing is concerned? Is there a newspaper? If so, what kind of writer and writing are they looking for? Who's in charge? Where and when are the editorial meetings? Is there a literary magazine or two? Who's in charge? Where and when are the editorial meetings? Do the people involved seem like people you'd like to hang out with, or not? Is there an improv troupe? A fantasy fiction gang? A bunch of people who put on live poetry slams? An unusually literate graffiti artist? Ask your teachers—they'll be glad to see you want to get involved.

Another way of thinking about campus is to remember that every writer needs something to write about. So where are your materials and your inspiration going to come from? If you're interested in movies, is there a film club? If you're interested in politics, what's going on in terms of student government? Is there student activism around issues that matter to you? Even something as fundamental as food: is there a foodie gang you might join? Nothing says that your new friends on campus have to be writers.

Here's the thing: until now, "writing" has probably meant, in your mind, one or two different kinds of writing—papers for school, maybe poetry, maybe fiction, maybe some journalism. But writing is actually an incredibly broad and diverse range of activities, skills, and interests, and part of your job is to broaden your horizons to get a sense of what, out of all the infinite possibilities, most appeals to you.

The trick is to check things out, even if the first time you just sit at the back and say nothing. The other thing to remember is that every generation of writers will move on, and it needs its successors. Never assume you're too young, too inexperienced, or not a good enough writer.

Join an on-campus club

I've read it everywhere (so it must be true) that students who have a higher level of involvement in their campuses outside of the classroom excel more in class and feel a deeper connection to the school and to everyone around them. It pays off for you to get involved in the things that are going on around campus that aren't required by a class.

Getting involved allows you to meet other students who have similar interests, so you can expand your conversation and your social circle. If the only time you venture onto campus is to go to class, then the only people you're ever going to meet are the kids in your classes. And even though those students are mostly going to be in your major, they could have very different interests than you do, and you may not connect with them beyond the surface level. As much as no one wants to think of it, you could be the black sheep of your major: joining a club and getting involved outside of your academic life could give you the sense of belonging that you're missing in the classroom, and it will make a huge difference to your collegiate experience.

Depending on the type of club or organization that you choose to join (and you should join as many as are interesting to you so long as you don't overcommit your limited time and energy), there are also opportunities to expand your academic knowledge in fun and interesting ways. Clubs give you the opportunity to connect your learning with practical, real-life experiences that you may not get to experience while in a classroom setting, and they could expand your range of interests and open your eyes to new experiences that you may never have thought of before.

There are a lot of different types of clubs and campus activities that you could join. Even the non-literary activities offer writing opportunities. When our college's Running Club set up its own website, it needed a writer/blogger, and one writing major after another discovered blogging and social media skills through that club website.

Writing opportunities are everywhere. I can't walk down the street without finding one. It's all about knowing where to find them and finding the motivation inside yourself to write about the things that you find. And if you should stumble upon something that interests you but doesn't seem to be about writing at all, make it about writing. No one's going to stop you.

Amanda King

You never know where the smallest opportunity may lead you. At the beginning of my first semester, I went to a student newspaper meeting. I spent most of it feeling lost and out of place. I didn't even have an idea for what to write until mid-way through the meeting. At the end, I got up and asked the Editor-in-Chief if I could write a gay history column. I was shaking and I'm sure my voice was at the wrong pitch for me but, 10 minutes later, I had my column.

The next semester, I was asked to be the Columns Editor. Basically, my job would entail recruiting columnists, editing their stories, and enforcing deadlines. I was afraid and not at all confident in my editing abilities, but I took the job. I was offered the position again for the fall semester of my sophomore year. At the end of that semester, I was offered a list of promotions ranging from Managing Editor and Dublin Correspondent to Editor-in-Chief. I immediately accepted all of them.

Towards the end of it, I was offered the chance to attend a conference at the *New York Times* for student editors of college papers. I went with two other girls, had a wonderful time, and am currently being paid to write a press release about my experience.

Meet the other writers on campus

I am going to introduce you to a mind-blowing idea, so I want you to sit down first.

Get to know your professors.

No, not just get to know. Build a relationship with them. Sometimes we see professors as necessary evils, but that's a high school mentality, and it can lead you to miss out on a lot. You shouldn't be afraid to talk to your professors and ask them about their experiences. They're people who have years of experience in journalism, publishing, poetry, radio, you name it. Take the initiative and ask them questions. Go ahead and take advantage of their office hours to pick their brains. The right professor could be your mentor, your colleague, even your friend. If you step it up, and put dedication into your work, maybe they'll even share their list of contacts with you and, when the time comes, write you the recommendation that may get you your first gig.

You are going to a school where there are writers on your campus, roaming around freely. There are writers teaching your classes. There are writers visiting your classes. There are writers everywhere—published, accomplished writers who actually receive money for their writing. What a concept, I know.

These writers are going to be especially helpful to you because, by reading your work, they will get to know you on a personal level. They are going to know your strengths and weaknesses intimately. They are going to know what types of critiques work for you and what your learning style is. They are huge assets to you, so why not try to get some face-time outside of the classroom?

Erin Gleeson

I have attended weekly meetings with my poetry professor to discuss my work and to work on developing not only myself, as a writer, but also my stylistic choices and my versatility. This has allowed me to accept criticism, gain a confidence in my writing (where it belongs), and to recognize my weaknesses and how I can strengthen those skills. It has taught me to take chances, look back at my work, and recognize how I have changed as a writer and how I am growing as writer.

What is a writing class for?

We all come to school to learn. We all want to enter a class and take something meaningful away from it. If we thought we would learn nothing, then why bother, right? Yet there are students who think that they've already learned everything that they need to know about writing. They just need time to write, and maybe someone to tell them where a comma should go. Some student writers think that most classes are a waste of their time. I disagree 100 percent.

I don't want to get up on my high horse and preach to you about the importance of class. I am not your mother. I'm not going to keep a tally of the classes that you miss or the homework you didn't do. You are in college now and it's your job to take responsibility for your education. If you want to take a passive role in your education and you're content to simply skate by unnoticed, and all you want is the diploma to put on your resume, that's fine by me. But for those of you who are interested in hearing some examples of how class isn't just a waste of your time and isn't just something that professors use to torture you, then please, read on.

I'll use myself as an example. I have always struggled with transitions between description and dialogue in my writing. I always seemed to have either too much description or too much dialogue, and I've never been able to find that middle ground. That is, until I took Creative Writing and I was introduced to my latest muse, Robert Owen Butler. He wrote this little book called *From Where You Dream* in which he talked about a type of daydream writing where you sit down and write everything that you need to say or do to tell your story on note cards. I was skeptical, but I thought it couldn't hurt to give it a shot.

It has done wonders for my writing. Now when I write, I take one piece of paper and write down all the dialogue that I need to tell the story. I put the paper away and walk away from the project, eat some food, sleep, whatever, and then I take out a fresh piece of paper and write down all the actions that I need. After that, I take out the two pieces of paper and combine them. I put the action where it needs to be to accompany the dialogue, add action where it's missing (though I try not to), and dialogue where it's missing (I try not to do this, too). It takes a little while longer, but most things that are worth the effort do take longer. All this improvement because of one class.

You are probably going to take at least one class that you just don't like and that you are not interested in. You are going to take a class that takes deep inner strength to get through and that you drag your feet to get to the end of. And maybe you won't learn anything and the experience of being in that class won't be valuable to you at all. Maybe you will think that it was a complete waste of your time. But maybe you'll go from being uninvested in the work you're producing to creating something marvelous. Maybe the class that you think you are going to hate will surprise you.

And then won't you feel silly for thinking that class was only good for naps?

Alli Neal

Having to write a minimum of 168 pages in one semester meant that I couldn't just write when I thought I had something good—which, honestly, meant I didn't write often. I had to start thinking like a writer. I had to start writing like a writer.

The best thing this class did for my writing was to, for the first time, make me feel like a writer...it changed the way I go about writing. Instead of mulling something over until it was final-draft quality before putting it on paper and losing half of it between my mind and my pen, I learned how to get down all the crap first. I learned how to pick the decent stuff out of the crap and play with it until it was good. I learned how to stop thinking and just write.

Grades: do they matter?

Maybe you had the kind of high school career where you did your best to get good grades in every subject. Maybe you did well at some classes (including writing, you'd hope) but could never get the hang of math or Spanish. Whatever the case, that's largely in the past now, as far as your writing career is concerned. Your high school grades have been good enough to get you into college—what now?

Let's start with the bottom line. You probably need to maintain a given GPA (usually 2.0) just to stay in college. Before things start to get even close to that bad, though, your teachers and your advisor are going to start noticing and start worrying, and will be knocking on your door to find out what's going wrong and how they can help.

In the end, the question needs to be turned around: it's not a question of whether grades matter; it's whether your writing matters. If you set out to be the best writer you can be, to take some risks, to get the most out of your time at college, then even if you still struggle with math and Spanish, your grades will be okay. More importantly, your writing will be more than okay, and that's what will give you the deepest satisfaction and the greatest change of finding a worthwhile and stimulating way ahead.

It's really, really unlikely that when you're hoping for a writing gig, any potential employers will want to know your GPA. Things they will look at are:

* **Samples of your writing.** Even if the samples are slightly different from what they will want you to do, they want to know if you can write a strong, interesting sentence.

* **Evidence that you can come up with your own ideas** and create your own projects, which also means evidence that you can follow through and finish what you start.

* **Signs that you have practical experience** closely related to the gig you're applying for. This often means a strong recommendation from your internship supervisor.

* **Recommendations** and/or testimonials from your teachers, your advisor, your program director. They're the ones who know your grades, and future employers will want to see that you've really got a lot out of college, especially out of your writing classes. They'll

also want to see evidence that you've committed to your work and respected their teaching. But they know that everyone is human, that we all have ups and downs, and if you take risks, you're going to be just a little erratic at times.

Mike Garris

Write for yourself. No matter what you do, whether it's blogging, writing short stories, or writing novels, do it for yourself. If you do it to get famous, or make money, when it doesn't happen right away you are going to get disappointed, and that can be really, really discouraging. So when you write, do so for your own satisfaction and let the readers come to you.

No, you won't have a secretary

I am a terrible speller. I know that I'm a terrible speller. I accept that I'm a terrible speller. I also have three copies of the Merriam-Webster dictionary (one on the desk in my bedroom, one on the living room coffee table, and one on the kitchen table) and the online edition bookmarked on my computer. I know how to use that dictionary, even if I haven't the slightest idea how to spell a word.

You don't have to memorize every word that you come into contact with. You don't need to know the place of origin of the word (although if you learn enough about roots and etymology, your spelling will improve tremendously). You don't even need to know how many syllables are in it. You do need to know what a dictionary is and how to look up words in it. Do not rely on spell check to find your mistakes. I'll repeat it: Do not rely on spell check for anything. It could be the biggest mistake you make.

The second biggest mistake you could make would be to hand in something that has spelling mistakes in it. This goes for giving things to your professors, your friends, your parents, or God forbid, a publication. It could be the next Pulitzer Prize-winning work, a pure stroke of genius, and you will still not be taken seriously as a writer if your spelling is awful.

I don't want to insult you by saying that you don't proofread your work and by telling you that you should proofread your work, but—proofread your work. If you aren't sure if something is spelled right, look it up. The 30 seconds it will take you to find the word in the dictionary is much less strenuous than the embarrassment you'll face when your professor hands back an assignment that has "begin" spelled wrong (because I've done that).

Words are a writer's tool, and unless you can spell and punctuate well (or use the dictionary well enough to cleverly disguise your lack of spelling

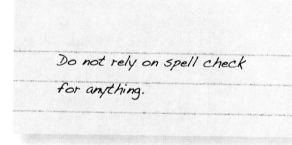

Do not rely on spell check for anything.

expertise), you are never going to be able to express yourself as well as you'd like. If you don't know how to use a word properly or spell it, you won't be able to use it, and you're limiting your vocabulary to only those words that you can spell and use in an intelligent way in a sentence. Your third biggest mistake would be to throw around words that you don't know how to use. Everyone who reads your piece is going to see right through that disguise and you'll lose some credit as a writer for it. Just don't do it.

You've got to take the technical side of writing seriously. You can be as creative as you want to be, but if you can't get those words down in an intelligent way, you aren't going to make it very far in your writing career. Make the dictionary your friend, expand your vocabulary, and proofread like a maniac. If you can't do those things, you might as well say, "I'm going to be a guitarist, and get someone else to tune my guitar for me." Yeah, go try that one and see how it works out for you.

While I said that you don't need to go out and memorize every word in the English language, there are some words that you should try to learn to spell. Check out the list of the 100 most commonly misspelled words. You can take a look at the list at your own discretion (a word I had to look up to spell, by the way), but do take a look at the list. If you can spell the words that most people can't, then you've suddenly put yourself ahead of the game. And that is exactly where you want to be.

The more you learn about language and how to use it, the more interesting you'll find it. Maybe you'll become an etymologist, who knows. And again, you don't need to become a spelling expert, but you don't want to be bordering on illiteracy, either.

Plus, let's face it: it'll be a while before you can afford a secretary.

David Ducey

Suffering builds character. This phrase is never truer than when applied to writing.

On the subject of spelling...

...I have some painful news for you. You're not only going to have to take spelling seriously, you're going to have to take grammar and punctuation seriously.

All those annoying bits and pieces you've been successfully avoiding since fifth grade—apostrophes, quotation marks, semicolons, verb tenses, dangling modifiers, split infinitives—well, it turns out they're the tools of your trade. You may have been able to get by with only the vaguest understanding of them so far, but then again, if you're a soccer player you can probably get away with being only half in shape and playing almost exclusively with your dominant foot while you're still in high school. At college, you're playing with the big dogs: those limitations are just going to make you look clumsy, and nobody who knows anything is going to take you seriously. You've got to start playing with both feet, with your head, with every tool, weapon, and device at your disposal.

What's more, you may have to make that decision and carry it through all on your own. Your college or university may not require you to take some kind of freshman course that forces you to brush up those skills, so you may get suckered into thinking you don't need to do anything about them, but let me tell you: once you start taking serious writing courses taught by serious writers, you'll get called out for making mistakes you don't even know you've made. Best to take the initiative yourself. Here are a few suggestions for how you might do that:

* **Pay attention to grammar check.** It's not going to catch all your mistakes, but those wiggly underlines are there for a reason. Don't just ignore them—make it your business to find out what they mean.

* **Ask your teachers to explain the markup they do on your writing.** It's very possible they regard basic written English skills as something you should have learned by sixth grade and are damned if they'll spend class time teaching them, but on the other hand, if you show you want to learn something, most teachers will respond.

* If you're really struggling, **make a regular weekly appointment at the campus Writing Center**. And remember: you're there not just to make sure you avoid a failing grade on the assignment, you're there to learn skills that are the tools of your trade and will help you for the rest of your life.

* And that leads into the most important and useful mind-set of all: **develop pride in your work**. You should want your writing to express exactly, not just more or less, what you mean. You should want people to be struck by every single thing you write, to pay attention to you, to regard you as someone who really, really knows what you're doing. Amina Srna, one week into an internship with a prestigious magazine in New York City, wrote back to us: "To be honest, I'm not too thrilled about the quality of the publication. I am finding that the writers are

sub-par and the Editor-in-Chief consistently misses errors in pieces and writes dull and uninformative pieces herself." In her freshman year, Amina's own writing had its share of basic technical mistakes, but she worked hard on that aspect of her craft, and look at the result: she's not only able to shine in a highly competitive environment, but she has the chops to end up as an Editor-in-Chief herself.

Get organized

If there's one thing I can advise you on with complete confidence, it's organization. Call me anal if you want. You can say that you think organization stifles creativity and keeps you from being spontaneous, but just don't waste your breath trying to tell me that you think it's unnecessary. I don't often tell people that they're wrong, but if you think you don't need organization to succeed as a writer, you're wrong.

I have my entire life color coded. While still in school, I had a colored binder for each class with a matching folder and accompanying highlighter so that I would know exactly what homework was due for each class. I even had colored Post-Its so I would know what I needed to do each day for each class. And if you think that's a little obsessive, you can't argue with the results: I am the most likely person to win an award for handing everything in on time, and I have never had to pull an all-nighter in my life.

I wasn't always like this. In junior high and the very beginning of high school, I didn't own a single notebook. I stuffed my backpack full of loose-leaf paper and a single pencil and would just pull things out at random in class to take notes. While that seems fun and funny now, it was not practical, and it was not productive. I would come home at the end of the day and spend at least half an hour trying to figure out which notes belonged to which class and what order they went in, and what the homework due tomorrow was. It was…stressful.

I'm sure those of you who have spent your high school experience in a state of disorganization are going to feel more than a little overwhelmed upon arrival on campus. The homework is more spaced out and demanding than in high school, and the professors are not going to remind you of the homework constantly. What was once stressful can easily become overwhelming. Disorganization is the single most common cause for failure in your first year. Besides, there's nothing more embarrassing than not handing in the homework when everyone else has.

So I am going to provide you with some quick steps to take to get yourself organized.

* **Get yourself a planner.** A daily planner, not a weekly or monthly one. You want to have space to write down the homework for each class, your work schedule, and any social events that you have to attend. Basically, you want to leave space to write down anything that you might not remember to do but need to keep track of. So a pocket-sized planner just won't do. You need the real deal.

* **Buy a calendar and find an open space on your wall to hang it up.** The type of calendar that you buy doesn't matter. I'm personally a fan of the erasable calendar, but if you want one with optical illusions or pictures of swimsuit models, that's fine, too, so long as you can write on it. Also, it's probably the easiest to hang the calendar above your computer or desk, in a place where you are sure to see it every day. Don't try to cram it in between your posters of the Grateful Dead and Phish, and then be surprised when you don't remember to look at it. This calendar is for the most important events: exams, doctor's appointments, your girlfriend's (or boyfriend's) birthday. Things that just aren't acceptable to forget. Of course, write these things in your planner as well, but you're most likely to skim over them buried among your daily homework and obligations. I've found it's best to have a back-up for the essentials.

* **Buy yourself some pens and pencils.** And a place to store those pens and pencils. You can buy all the planners and calendars in the world, but if you don't have a writing utensil to record in them with, they are useless. A pen that doesn't work is as useless as not having

one, which is why it's important to carry multiples with you. One of the worst things you can do is arrive at a writing class without something to write with, or on, so don't be that person. And I say to buy something to put them in because I am prone to losing things—most of all small things like pens—so carrying around a holder for them helps me to keep track of where they are. Plus, it gives me a lovely flash of nostalgia for the Lisa Frank pencil case I had in grade school.

* **Remember to actually write down everything that you are likely to forget and need to remember.** It's slightly ridiculous that I have to write this step down, but I'm afraid that if I didn't, some people wouldn't remember this most crucial of steps. Don't tell yourself that you are going to write it down later, either. Write down everything as soon as you can. Sometimes it's impossible to write it down immediately, but try to write it down as early as you can so you don't forget about it. We've all had that moment where you sit down and think, "What was I supposed to remember?" The goal of organization is to limit the number of these moments.

Additional optional steps:

* **Give yourself false deadlines.** Especially if you are prone to pulling all-nighters before a big assignment is due, it may be helpful to set yourself smaller, false deadlines along the way. Planners are also helpful for breaking down how long you have to complete an assignment, especially because they make it easier to compare your workload on a day-to-day basis, so being organized and writing it all down can help you to be more deadline-oriented as well. Organize your workload into manageable amounts for each night so you don't end up putting in 10 hours of work in the wee hours of the morning (because your work never ends up as good as you think it is at the time). Which leads to...

* **Organize your workload using Post-Its and to-do lists.** The only way I function is to make to-do lists for each day. At the top is my work schedule for that day if I work, followed by the list of homework

assignments that are due the following day (crossed out if I've done them, because nothing is more fulfilling than crossing something out), anything social I have planned for that day and the time and location so I don't forget it, and finally, the list of things I would like to accomplish that day in addition to all the things already listed. For me, I used Post-It notes and highlighted everything to the class and color it belonged to because then I could stick it in my planner, but you may want to have an additional notebook if you have big writing or a lot of things you do in one day.

Which leads us to lucky number seven, the step I find the most important and the most helpful of all.

* **Color-coordinate.** I know that this one is a big stretch for most of you, but especially when it comes to classes, it's so helpful. If you're taking four or five classes in a semester, writing down "assignment one due" is going to get pretty confusing, and if all your classes are writing classes, writing down "turning point prose due" may also get old quick. Unless you've got a mind like an elephant, you are not likely to remember which generic assignment title corresponds with which class. You're more likely to remember that purple is Screenwriting and blue is Poetry.

If you follow my advice, you will be well on your way to usurping me and becoming the new Queen or King of Organization. At the very least, you will become a more organized, professional, and sane individual.

Mike Varraso

Check not only the due dates of assignments, but where you should post them. For example, if a professor asks you to [post some writing], and you blank on where it should go, well, that's bad. Plus, you look like an idiot when you're four days late and everyone else has done the assignment.

Be an observer

Getting to know your way around the campus may seem confusing or even overwhelming at first, so here's a trick: turn it into an exploration you're doing for yourself. Imagine yourself as an anthropologist or a visiting alien and make it your business to observe the natives at work and play.

This has a second advantage: it gives you all kinds of input. There's only just so much you can write about yourself, but there's an infinite amount you can write about other people. You are surrounded by raw material that you might turn into stories, essays, poems, plays, screenplays—almost anything.

In particular, watch how people move, what they do with their hands and their eyes. Listen to how they talk. These details, and these habits of observation, will last you for a writing lifetime.

Sarah Lucia

Be a lurker. Freshman year I wrote a section of dialogue for an assignment and the feedback was, "It's too much like a video game character. It doesn't sound real enough." So I went home and just eavesdropped. I listened to my brother talk to his friends over Xbox Live, I listened to the kids outside and I listened to my parents talk to each other. Of course, this was a lot easier for me because I'm an extremely curious and nosy person to begin with but the point of it isn't just to learn everybody's secrets, it's to listen to how they say it. Now, it's second nature. I'm always listening to people as they walk by, cataloging everything they say and how they say it. Dialogue is now one of my favorite things to write, and I really feel like I'm good at it and I know what I'm doing.

Share your work

It is important to share your work right out of the gate. As early as you can. If you sit in a classroom where no one shares their work with each other and the only person who lays their eyes on your work is the instructor, and especially if you never have to read your work out loud, there is no benefit to you. That kind of writing environment isn't going to help you improve as a writer.

Maybe you feel uncomfortable sharing your work. Maybe you would rather stick a hot needle into your eye, but you have to get over that fear, and the sooner you do that, the better writer you'll become for it.

Writing can be a lonely profession. You sit at home by yourself and you write. Maybe you write about the things you're afraid to say, or that you can't express in any other way. What you write is very personal. And it puts you in a vulnerable position to have to share your work with a bunch of kids that you don't necessarily know and who don't know the context by which you wrote the piece, and who may not understand the meaning that you were going for.

People are going to misinterpret your work sometimes. They're going to hate something you wrote that you love. Not everyone that you encounter is going to love absolutely everything that you write. That is an unreal expectation. And you know what? They shouldn't. Because not everything that you write is perfect. No first draft is perfect. Even what I'm writing right now has flaws in it and someone else may have to read over this piece in order to find them.

Your writing is very close to you. It's a part of you put down on paper. And since it's so close to you, it would be impossible for you to see all of the mistakes in it. You know what you meant to write so when you're looking it over, it's very likely that you'll see "thought" if you actually wrote "though." Someone else looking over your piece will help to find those tricky little errors.

Your writing should be shared. Isn't that why you became a writer? To invite an audience into the world of your imagination? So get to sharing already!

Melinda Gray

Live your life—and then turn it into a best-seller. My proudest literary accomplishment so far has been the work I've done on the book I am writing about my marriage and divorce. At first, I was afraid to write about it because of the shame and embarrassment I thought the story would bring me. I messed up big time, did a horrible thing, and thought that if anyone read what I had done, they would hate me forever. But I wrote the story anyway and was amazed by the results. Not only did I have a beautifully written story to tell, but I have a lesson to teach my readers, and my readers actually responded positively to my story. Instead of crying harlot and stamping a scarlet 'A' to my chest (which my ex-husband would have loved), my readers identified with me and my story, and some of them even sympathized with me!

So, please, be weird like me and the next time something terrible happens to you, think to yourself: Yay, now I have one more great thing to write about!

If you don't start sharing your work now, what makes you believe that come graduation, you'll magically feel comfortable sharing it?

College will provide you with plenty of opportunities to get out there and share what you've got with an audience of your peers and other people from the community. Attend these events. Listen to what people are doing and take away everything that you can. Bleed these events dry for inspiration. Shake out your nerves and get up behind the mic yourself. Expose yourself. Make yourself vulnerable to these people and then write about what that was like for you.

Workshop. Often. There are definitely people out there who don't like workshops or don't think that they are helpful. Some people think that students don't listen to the advice of other students and that conducting workshops is a waste of valuable class time. I think that those people just haven't been in the right kind of workshop. I think that they're very useful and that the students in your classes know you and your work the best, and can give an accurate and fair assessment of what will help you improve your piece and what won't. But I'm not going to tell you what to believe. Actively participate in a workshop, and see for yourself whether they work for you or not. And if they do, suck them dry for help.

Amina Srna

What you are learning is going to make you a significantly better writer. What they aren't teaching you is that you'll also need to master public speaking. If it's too late for you to take a class on it, don't fret. Throw yourself at every chance to read your stuff out loud. Take your poetry to hippy coffee shop readings, take care to present well in all of your classes, get your voice on the radio! As a writer, it's going to be up to you to promote your work. Get used to hearing your own voice, my kindred little spirit.

Be fearless

Sharing your work leads to the question of courage. Not only will you be asking yourself, "Is this good enough to show other people?" but pretty soon, if you're taking the kinds of risks a writer should take, you'll ask yourself, "If I show this to other people, won't they think I'm really, really weird?"

In high school, you probably wrote what your teachers told you to write, and that's fine. Maybe you took a writing class or two, but how much did you really get to express yourself and say the things that were interesting to you? Probably not a lot.

The fact is, you're not in high school now. It's time to take initiative with your writing. Now is the time to start writing about everything—every heartbreak, every date, every sexual encounter, every drug, every surprise—don't let any of it go. Your experiences will fuel your writing, so make sure you will always have somewhere to go back to and remember it.

Emma Devine

I spent the majority of my high school writing career limiting myself to bullshit topics. I would write about things that I really didn't care about, the things that didn't really matter to me. I would write about the way the rain hit the classroom window or what I had for dinner the night before. That isn't what I wanted to write about. I wanted to write about having sex, experimenting with drugs, out rallying the police in my Honda. But, I was too scared...I wish I had the balls to write about my real life. I wish my teachers hadn't prompted me to write about trees when what a young adult should be writing about is their real life.

You shouldn't be afraid to use your personal experiences to fuel your writing. First of all, writing about personal experience allows you to write about something that you know. It's all well and good to decide to write a piece about turkey hunting, but if you don't know anything about turkeys or hunting, your audience is going to see right through that façade no matter how good your writing is. So, it's best to stick to what you know (and learn new things as you go along). When you write about yourself, the setting and characters are already there for you, so all you have to do is modify them to make a story out of your experience.

Second, it gives something for the reader to relate to, something human to understand in your writing. By chronicling your experience with bulimia, talking about the first time you had sex, or the battle with your emotions you faced at your mother's funeral, you're tapping into similar experiences that the reader has had, or has wondered about.

All forms of self-expression reveal something about ourselves, but writing can reveal a lot more, and in a more specific and graphic way than most other forms. As a result, we all sooner or later start to wonder what other people will think when they read what we've written.

This can be terrifying. What if my mother reads this? What if my grandmother reads it? What will the other kids in class think? Suddenly, you're questioning all the words that you've put down on the page. That anxiety of what others will think—it's huge. It can stop us dead in mid-sentence. It can prevent us from writing anything at all. It certainly makes some writers avoid writing memoir, non-fiction, poetry or other forms that make them feel naked. Fiction becomes a way for the writer to tell his or her own story in disguise, and journalism, especially objective hard-news journalism, becomes a way of avoiding revealing anything about yourself at all.

Some writers never get beyond that fear of nakedness. Those who do, though, find that (a) they write with a power and fearlessness that can't be achieved any other way, and (b) the reactions of our readers are rarely as dramatic and extreme as we imagine. In fact, when we write with the power of the truth, our fearlessness becomes a force in itself, and the reader usually can't help respecting us.

Jaime Berry

I call my mother. Yes, she says, she did get the package. Yes, she says, she did read it. It was interesting, she says. "But I think..." she says, "I don't think I will show it to your grandmother."

I call my father. Yes, he says, he did get the package. Yes, he says, he did read it. It was interesting, he says, it was surprising. "But I think..." he says, "I don't know if you really want your grandparents reading this."

I call my lover. Yes, she says, she got the e-mail. Yes, she says, she did read it. It was awful, she says. "It makes me look awful..." she says, "and don't you mind everyone knowing about our sex life?"

"Honestly," I tell her, "I never thought about it."

Since arriving at college, since entering a world where teachers are only Kerry or Steve or Anthony, where we talk sex and genocide and phallic symbols, I have stopped filtering my writing. I have written shamelessly about sex and cigarettes, infidelity, loathing. I have written these things and read them, aloud. I have passed them in to be read, edited, inspected, and graded. I have never thought twice about it. It did not occur to me until

43

my mother and father were worrying over it that perhaps my grandparents should not be reading tales of my first B&E, of losing my virginity and sharing my girlfriend with the U.S. military. It did not occur to me that agreeing to publication was, in this instance, agreeing to make my sex life required reading.

I do think about it, now. Looking back, I'm surprised at all the secrets I let slip, at all the intimate details I didn't leave out. When I write now, I hesitate. I think about the fact that a professor will read this, that my peers will, that these things will be public knowledge. I hesitate. I could choose a different word, a different phrase, I could replace the specific with the abstract and blur the lines—but I don't. That is not who I was or who I am; I am not ambiguous. I am specific and blunt. I am honest. Now that I'm aware of that, I find myself writing even more honestly; I intentionally write about the things that I am most uncomfortable sharing.

Also, I sent copies of the book to both sets of grandparents. They also thought it was...interesting.

Practice, practice, practice

Nothing gets accomplished by sitting back on the couch thinking about writing. You actually have to write to get anything done. And no masterpiece was created in one night. It takes time and dedication to produce a piece of writing that you're proud of showing off. Of course we all know those people (and are sometimes guilty of being them) who put things off until the absolute last second and then boast about how "great" it came out. Great compared to what? If you have one of those "great" pieces, go back and take a look at it now. I'm sure it doesn't seem so good now that you have time to go back and take a second look at it. I am willing to bet that there are at least 10 things that you would change if you could. Most good things in life take time, and writing is no exception.

Everyone has his or her own way of practicing writing. The general rule

I've learned in school is that you should write every single day for at least a half an hour. Some days that half hour is going to drag by and other days it's going to seem like half a second. That's just the way the beast works. And I'm not suggesting that you listen to that rule and dedicate yourself to write from 6:00 am to 6:30 every morning, but it's not a bad idea to plan writing time into your schedule. If you plan it ahead, you know that you won't forget to write one day because it's already in your schedule. Don't be afraid to write at a time outside of your designated time slot, however. Write whenever inspiration hits you. But try to get in the habit of writing something each day so when you do have a breakthrough moment, you aren't out of practice.

Of course, this isn't a technique that is going to work for everyone. The point is to find something that works for you. Try out different things. See what you like, see what you hate. For a lot of authors that I know, keeping a diary or journal seems to help. Even though they are mostly thoughts that you share only with yourself and the paper, it helps to write down how you're feeling.

A journal also serves as a seed-bed for all kinds of bits and pieces—words, phrases, sentences, ideas—that flash through your mind and might otherwise be lost.

Alli Neal

Journaling may seem like that thing dreamy, pubescent girls do in pink, locking diaries, but you need to rid yourself of this notion immediately. Start writing down impressions of anything and everything you come across. Make connections. Daydream, and then write about it. If you come up with a couple of lines that could maybe sound poetic in the right light, jot them down. If you get angry, write a righteous rant. If you have a brilliant idea for a children's book, drop everything and write it.

Whose approval are you after?

I started out as a Paralegal Studies major. Two weeks into the semester I knew that becoming a paralegal wasn't the profession that was interesting to me—I was going to make the change and become a writer like I had always dreamed of being when I was a little girl. Excited about the brightness of my future, I called my mother and let her know the great news. To my surprise, she didn't share my enthusiasm.

"What are you going to do with a *writing* degree?" she asked, and then launched into a thousand questions about what my plans were for the future and how was I ever going to pay back my college loans by writing? And if all I was going to do with my life was write, why would I waste my time going to college? And, was I still going to graduate or was I going to drop out like my brother had? Blah, blah, blah. The point is, she didn't say one encouraging thing during that conversation. And I still managed to graduate.

It's quite possible that your parents have been a lot more supportive. But maybe you have a boyfriend or a girlfriend, a friend, a grandmother, or anyone else who just doesn't quite understand why you want to become a writer. Maybe they don't understand what a writing degree is going to teach you or what you're going to do with it career-wise after graduation. If you've ever been asked if you're trying to become the next Stephen King, then you've had a little taste of what my experience has been when I've told people that I'm a writing major. So, no, you aren't alone.

Chances are that you have at least one person in your life (and if you have only one then I'm extremely envious) who isn't supportive of you and your decision to become a writer. Sure, you can cut them out of your life, take their criticism personally, and question what you're doing for the rest of your life.

Or you can prove them wrong. You can make these next four years the most productive years of your life and light this place on fire, showing all the doubters that they were wrong about you not having a future. You can show them exactly what you can do with a writing degree.

Maybe I'm completely wrong about you and you come from a long tradition of writers who expect you to become a writer, too. Maybe you've grown up writing. Maybe you've had a pen in your hand since you were in the womb. Maybe you were a little writing protégé and now you're in college to show off your talent to all your classmates.

Maybe you want to piss your parents off. They always thought you were going to become a businessman and work in your father's company. Well now you're an adult and you're going to shove that writing degree in their face upon graduation.

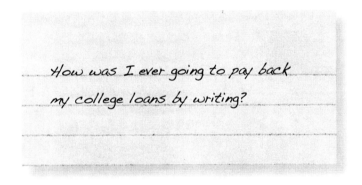

How was I ever going to pay back my college loans by writing?

Stop and think about it for a minute. Why did you become a writer? Who are you becoming a writer for? Is it yourself that you're trying to impress, or is someone else? For me, this is what I've wanted to do for a long time, but there's also this little menacing voice in the back of my mind that says, *Wouldn't it be great if I could prove my mother wrong about writing?*

This is a complicated issue. Maybe you aren't even aware of why you write. You just know that you have to write. There's a thirst deep inside of you that can only be quenched by writing. But if you think about it deeper, what's motivating you to write? Who's motivating you to write?

There was this guy who grew up in the same neighborhood that I grew up in, who went away to war and came home injured. I was home on break and ran into his mother, listened to her talk about him, and I knew in that moment that I had to write his story. He had a wonderful, inspiring, moving story that was trying to burst out of him, that he couldn't yet manage to tell for himself.

It was in writing his story that I first considered myself a writer. I put his words down on the page and I saw myself as having a rare skill. Helping him express his story helped me to see that I wasn't wasting my time as my mother would have me to believe, but that I was doing something that was going to make a difference to people.

When I changed my major to Professional Writing, I told myself that I was doing it for me, but now, three years later, I'm not sure how true that was. Of course I love to write and want to spend my life doing something that I love, so I want to become a writer for myself in that respect, but that is far from the only reason that I want to write. I would be lying if I said that my mother's approval wasn't important to me and that I've stuck with it in an effort to show her that I'm not wasting time and money. I always want to show that boy from my neighborhood that he was right to entrust his story to me and that I'm qualified to tell it.

Now, whose approval are you after?

Mike Perry

When you write, be yourself.

At the beginning of last semester, I was having trouble coming up with things to write about and whenever I would finish a piece, it just wouldn't sound right to me and I was never happy with anything I wrote. It turns out, I was writing to please the audience and I was writing about things that I haven't even experienced before. This was pointed out to me in my Creative Writing class and I am grateful for it. I was told that I should write about things I know and write straight from my mind and throw it onto the page and forget about if my reader would like it or not it. I didn't even realize that I was doing that—it was something I was doing subconsciously. When you write, just be yourself and forget about pleasing anyone else.

Anticipate disaster

At some point over the next four years, you'll suffer at least one computer-related disaster. You will:

* lose your USB drive

* have your external hard drive stolen

* accidentally erase 20 pages of your best writing

* save the wrong version of a major piece of work, thereby deleting all your most recent revisions

* acquire a virus that trashes your hard drive

* spill coffee all over your equipment, shorting out and frying your motherboard

* drop your laptop onto concrete

This disaster will be exquisitely painful, and the recovery impossibly tedious, but all in all it will be a very good thing because it will teach you the most important lesson of writers in the computer age: BACK UP YOUR WORK.

I'll say that again: BACK UP YOUR WORK.

Not just every few days—every few sentences.

A quick tip: when you're writing something valuable, save it every single paragraph, and as soon as you come to a pausing-point, email it to yourself. That way it's saved on the email server. Twice, in fact—in both your Sent mail folder and in whatever folder you create for drafts of your own writing.

One more time: BACK UP YOUR WORK.

And if, by some miracle, you graduate from college without a single computer-related catastrophe, don't assume you've dodged the bullet: the bullet is just waiting for the moment when it can shoot down the first seven chapters of your novel. Never assume it won't happen to you. It will. There is only one course of action that will save you. Ya gotta back up your work.

Writing well is the best revenge

Remember the insufferable roommate, the guys playing the beer pong marathon? The great advantage you have as a writer is that you can turn them into fame and fortune for yourself by writing about them. In the *Buffy* series, Joss Whedon created an insane monster roommate who really was an insane monster (well, a demon from another dimension, anyway). Ali Wisch has written two hysterically funny plays about 20-something slackers who still have that college-dorm mentality, one of which opens with two guys playing beer Battleship.

So turn the novelty and the mayhem of your college life to your advantage. Listen hard, and take good notes.

Abby Messick

Never, ever, ever work in close proximity to a TV.

Back up your work and save often!

Second Year

Okay. You've survived your first year, and with a bit of luck you even have some interesting scars to show and stories to tell. Now your feet feel more grounded, it's time to start expanding your horizons, exploring, taking risks—in all kinds of ways.

Your second year is when you start to move beyond just doing writing as a reflexive act, and start thinking about writing. It's the first significant step in moving away from being a writing student and toward being a writer.

You're starting to realize that writing is a set of skills and a process, and you're thinking that it might be smart to understand how those skills and that process work. Instead of asking, "What's the assignment?" you start asking, "What do I really want to write about?" and "How am I going to do my best work?"

Jocellyn Harvey

Share your work in an open forum. Go to every reading possible. Take time off of work, go to dinner late, and rush to one during your class break. Writing can become a very lonely, solitary task, but sharing your work out loud will make you feel better. Until then, you might be just writing to a teacher or writing to yourself, which can seem like you aren't going anywhere. Reading out loud instills you with this great responsibility. You consciously work harder to make sure the pieces you are sharing are the best they can be. You'll practice them beforehand and tweak them as you go. You're going to work damn hard in this major, and it's only fair you get to share.

And always, always, always remember to remain humble.

Start picking your classes

You've chosen a major that gives you a lot of freedom. Some programs have barely any electives at all. Now, are you going to take advantage of that rare perk?

The answer is yes, you are. You are not going to sit around and wait for your professors and the director of the major to tell you what classes you should take (with the exception of required classes, which are required for a reason and you are going to have to take those, fortunately and unfortunately). You are going to decide for yourself what classes you would like to take.

Are you going to take classes just because all your writing friends are taking them? Probably. But you shouldn't. To use that old cliché, would you jump off a bridge because all your friends are doing it? Some of you would, and you shouldn't do that, either. You should be taking the classes that you want to take because you want to take them, not because all of your roommates want to take them and you are scared to be in a class where you don't know anyone. It might be a blessing in disguise if you are the only person you know in the class. If that's the case, you can make any sort of impression you want.

You don't want to suddenly be a senior and realize that you always wanted to take Food Writing or Playwriting, but now you don't have time to take it. The glory about only being in your second year is that you still have four or five semesters to pick your classes and make sure that you are able to take the classes that are interesting to you. This also gives you time to research the classes that are available to you, and petition the people that you need to petition to get permission to take classes outside of the major that you think may help you in your future endeavors.

Get out of your comfort zone

Your field of interest is going to be severely limited if you don't push yourself out of your comfort zone. In order to succeed in life, and in your writing, you are going to have to take some risks. Sometimes they'll back-fire, but sometimes they'll really pay off. And how are you to ever know the difference if you don't put yourself out there?

Ashley DeFelice

I think the biggest thing that contributed to my development as a writer happened last semester, in my Creative Non-Fiction class, when we were told to write memoirs. I usually write almost exclusively fiction and poetry. Even when I journal, I'm more likely to talk about how I feel rather than what went on in the day. When I write, I'm more likely to make up events, however real they seem to the story, than to concentrate on putting down anything totally factual. So, this was my first time doing anything remotely memoir-y, and I gained a lot from it. I realized that there is a line between fiction and nonfiction. I found out that I was able to write a good 30 pages without feeling finished, and without feeling that if anyone ever read it, they'd be terribly bored. I learned that writing doesn't have to be even close to chronological to tell a story, and sometimes it's the most powerful that way.

Stay interested in your writing

Writing is like having a relationship: it requires commitment above everything else. You may love the person you're with, but you may also get into a fight and you won't like them very much tomorrow. But you aren't going to break up over one fight (depending on the fight) or stay mad forever—you'll make up and then you'll be lovey-dovey and happy once again. The same thing goes for writing.

In the beginning, everything is going wonderfully and you can't write fast enough to keep up with the thoughts that are coming to you, practically bursting out of your head onto the pages. You want to spend all your time writing because you have to get those words out. But then you hit a wall. What's going to happen after your star storms away from her parents, swearing never to return? Where is your story going to go from there? Suddenly, your mind is blank. You think about giving up and moving onto a bigger and better piece whose idea has been festering in the back of your mind for some time. You start to doubt the piece that you're writing. Maybe it isn't such a good idea after all. So, you can give up, or you can stick by that story that you were absolutely in love with last week and work through the rough patch to find a solution to the problem.

I have confidence that you'll find, as with relationships, that a story is more rewarding to write when you complete it. No story wants to be abandoned in the middle, just like a relationship seems a waste of time if there isn't some sort of closure about it. Every story wants to be written from beginning to end, and you'll get nothing out of it if you leave it unfinished at the first sign of something that you don't like.

When you start a story, you need to stay committed to it because there is a solution to every roadblock that you'll face. There is an answer to all the questions that keeping popping up as you write. There's an ending in that story that you're working on somewhere. The key is to find it, and to stay focused and determined until you find it.

Then, once the story is finished, it's perfectly all right to take a look at it and decide that it isn't the story for you, and put it away for good.

At least you learned a little bit about what you want (or don't want) in a story in the future, right?

There are a lot of different ways to go about maintaining your focus and interest on the piece that you're working on. You can always take a break from your piece, take a walk outside, take a shower, make yourself a meal, and then return to the story later on with a fresher view and some new ideas to explore. Talk about it with friends and bounce ideas off of them. Just be cautious with this so that your piece doesn't turn into something other than what you want it to be.

I said it before and I'll say it again, commitment is the key to success when it comes to writing. You have to muscle through some of those hard times and stay with it, or else you'll end up with a hundred half-written pieces and nothing complete.

Think outside your writing box

In high school and even in your first year of college, you tend to think of the words "writing" and "writer" in terms of the writing you've done or studied in class—and that's a pretty narrow range of genres. Some fiction, some poetry, maybe some journalism. It's very easy to assume that if you want to be a writer, that's what you'll need to do. In most English courses, in fact, writers (especially poets and fiction writers) are held up as gods, and as a student you're almost bound to start thinking, "Yes! Some day that could be me!"

The danger here is that if you're not particularly interested in poetry and not particularly good at fiction, you start doubting yourself as a writer and thinking you should maybe change to dentistry, especially if your friends and/or family have been telling you all along that you'd never make a living as a writer.

The truth is, writing is not one profession, but a thousand. What's more, writing is also a significant part of a thousand other professions. Much of your time at college, then, needs to be spent exploring just who you are as a wrier, and what kinds of writing you enjoy and want to pursue.

Emma Crockett

I used to look at writing as this narrow, traditional, and elite profession. I thought that novelists were the truest, most respectable writers on Earth, and becoming a novelist was it for me. That was my goal. Above all, I saw it as an easy out. I figured I'd write a novel, sell it, and live off the royalties. I can't believe I was that naive. Or that egotistical.

Writing, I've realized, is not just one thing, it's many. A novelist is no better than a poet, a playwright, or a screenwriter. And for all you introverts like me, watch out: writing doesn't take place in a vacuum like we had hoped. After the words have been put on the page, many hands get involved. The agent, the editor, the publisher, the marketer, the bookseller: all working in tandem to get your writing to the world.

Being a writer is about an eighth of the romance you expect, and about seven times more hard work and dedication.

You have to get it out of your head that you have to write a bestselling novel or else. It'll just psych you out. And stop confining yourself to the genre or form you've become accustomed to. I've started to realize that maybe I will never be a novelist. I'd prefer to become a screenwriter.

Put yourself online

We are in the age of technology. There are hundreds of different ways that you can utilize the Internet and get your writing out there for people other than your classmates and professors to read:

* You can join or create writing groups.

* You can invent new forms of multi-dimensional or multi-media writing, or interactive writing.

* You can develop and manage a fan base and, conversely, you can

contact some of your favorite writers and pick their brains.

* You can create a professional portfolio.

* You can blog for a club or a non-profit organization that is important to you.

* You can blog about your favorite subjects and develop not only writing skills but subject knowledge and a devoted readership.

* You can publish long pieces of writing, such as novels, in serial form.

* You can even start earning an income by writing for and editing other people's websites.

What's more, the fastest-growing area of jobs for writers is on the Web. As with everything else, the earlier on in your writing career that you explore these venues and develop much sought-after Internet skills, the easier it will be to land that job upon (or even before) graduation.

For now, you don't need to commission a custom-made website (which can easily set you back $5,000—$10,000), and you don't even need mad Web skills. It's perfectly okay to start at the blog level.

You may think of yourself as a technophobe, but if you can manage a Facebook account, you can manage a blog. A basic blog format has limitations and, as you become more Web-literate, you'll probably want to move up to a WordPress site or something along those lines, as that will allow you more flexibility and a clearer sense of identity. But for now, you can dip your toe into the waters of the Internet without fear of drowning. It's actually far easier to learn how to make a website work than to learn how to make best use of it.

When you start a blog, a lot of the traffic you'll receive and the audience you'll build will be with people whom you don't know and have never met. You could also call them strangers. The thing that's both good and bad about writing for strangers is they don't know you personally, so they can be brutally honest with their opinions on your work. Can it be heartbreaking? Yes, of course, but it's also extremely helpful.

Strangers are people who can look at your work objectively, which is especially helpful if you are planning to write for the general public post-graduation. It will help you get into the habit of writing for people other than yourself, your friends or your professors. Unlike things you've written in high school, or assignments that you've turned in for a college grade, blogging is writing you do because you know someone is going to read it.

Sometimes you'll find that the process even works in reverse. Just as you can inspire your audience, your audience can inspire you.

Carissa Stimpfel

Originally, in its (and my) immature stages, Sex and the College Girl was something of an online diary. After an extremely abrupt maturation period toward the end of October, I started to catch on to something that had been eluding me: if you have followers (AKA: blog readers), you have the ability to affect other people, create change, and at the very least, make someone feel less alone or alienated.

It started with a post called "All My Single Ladies." I received more comments on that singular post about appreciating the beauty and self-strength that is being a single girl than on any I had written before. What touched me most was an extremely simple comment—all it said was "Thank you so much for this." This started the cogs in my head churning. It went something along the lines of this: "You mean...blog readers...connecting to material...means...a more appreciated blog? Better traffic? More readers? Being held responsible to a higher standard of writing and not talking down to readers?"

Since then, I have struggled and done my best to provide a blog that melds the frankness of the female college-age experience with the human touch that out there, someone else is experiencing the same exact thing, and maybe they don't have the words or ability to voice them like I do. My readers have become more to me than just people who comment—they are now real friends, people whom I check in with monthly to get the scoop on their lives, and other women asking for advice, an opinion, or

> just someone to hear them out. Something that started
> out—yes—selfishly is now something that provides me
> with an outlet to reach others.

Writing is a two-way street. On one side is you, the writer, but on the other is the reader, and you should make it your mission to cross paths with the other side as often as possible.

The more places that people can come into contact with your name and see your work, the more popular you'll become. I'm sure you've all heard the phrase, "All publicity is good publicity." Well, this is true for you as well. Get yourself out there. Get involved with others who share your interests in the Internet world.

If you are on Facebook, put a link to your latest blog post in your status. Tell all your friends about your blog. Check out the forum scene and join one that interests you. Make friends with those individuals who share your interests, and tell them about your blog. Tell your mother and your father (unless you're writing about them, in which case you may want to work gradually up to full public disclosure!) and have them tell their friends. Be shameless.

If you can manage a Facebook account, you can manage a blog.

In addition to blogs, there are more professional sites that can help you become better known within the writing profession, or within areas of your own specific interest.

Through LinkedIn, for example, you can connect with other writers and get feedback from the professionals in the field. You can also get people to post recommendations on your behalf—just what you want your potential editor or employer to see! This is not to say that blog followers are not knowledgeable and that their feedback isn't worthwhile, but there is also something satisfying about having a working professional writer praise your work.

Another nice thing about being a writer is the ability to use a pseudonym. I happen to like my name and think it has a lovely little ring to it, but if your writing is something that you don't want your mother to connect you with, or you've always hated the name given to you on your birth certificate, you can change it to anything you'd like it to be. Did you know that Anne Rice was born Howard Allen O'Brien? So, really, there is nothing to worry about when putting yourself online.

Get cracking.

Choose your topic

Let's suppose you're primarily a short-story writer, but you also have an interest in photography and you'd like to write food reviews. Should you do them all on the same site, or should you reserve one site for your stories and create different sites for the other two?

There are no hard and fast answers. Sometimes you want a site with many dimensions so visitors will wander from one to another; sometimes you want to create a very specific focus, especially if the look or feel of one of your projects might clash with another.

You may also consider how often you're planning to post on each topic. If you post frequently on one subject but keep another static, almost as a kind of portfolio, you may want to separate the two.

Embedding audio, video, music, sound effects, flashing lights, etc., like any stylistic device, are all techniques that you can learn easily how to use; it's more a question of whether to use them. What works well for a heavy metal site may not fit with a site where you plan to write book reviews.

Let's consider a specific example. Poetry, which traditionally was a live and public art form, has developed a curiously ambivalent attitude toward its public. On the one hand, it has become a serious poet's greatest ambition to be published in small periodicals with even smaller circulations, as if readership were a corrupting influence. Seen this way, it would seem entirely askew to create a site for your poetry that draws too much attention to itself. On the other hand, the rise of slam poetry has busted open the doors of the academic-intellectual complex and taken poets to the streets and the stage—so why not adopt the same attitude on the Web?

The great thing about a blog is that it doesn't restrict you to conventional forms of writing. A blog is yours—you are the publisher. Like any publisher, you can, and should, publish whatever is important to you and may be interesting and valuable to others.

You probably still have a lot of questions about online writing—questions that are well worth exploring. Does a blog cheapen my writing? Will serious writers look down at me? If I publish my work online, does that mean I then can't publish it in print?

Frankly, we can't answer those questions because the way people use and regard blogs is changing almost by the day. Three years ago, almost no established authors had their own web pages or chatted online with their readers; now a variety of highly-regarded and popular writers use the Web in a far more open way without feeling as if they're cheapening themselves.

Writing is about starting a conversation. Using the Web means you can write as all the best writers write—in order to affect people. And when they respond, you can see how you have affected them. While some will disagree with your point of view or dislike your style, this is all part of the adventure of being a public writer—which, unless you plan to spend the rest of your life hiding your stories in a drawer or showing them only to your best friend, is where you're headed. Having a Web presence simply gets you there sooner, and makes the conversation happen more readily.

Michael Sheerin

If I, a lazy, insomniac slacker, can network myself, then there's really no reason or excuse for anyone else not to be able to. However, my advice doesn't just apply to networking, it applies everywhere. I would advise all newer writers in the program to show their work to all who'll read it. Not because they're hoping for a good review—quite the opposite, actually. They should hope for some good, old fashioned grating criticism, so that they might have an opportunity to learn from it. Though writers are often some of the most introverted people, shyness is not a luxury they can afford.

Meet writers off campus

Unless you go to a school located in the middle of a field or a desert, there is going to be some kind of off-campus writing scene going on all around you.

In your second year, you need to start broadening your range. You've been around long enough to hopefully be aware of, and involved in, the writing scene going on around campus, so now it's time to go out and see the world a bit. If you only write about your own interests, and you only ever meet people who are doing the same thing as you, you're going to develop a very limited sense of what is interesting, what is important, and what is possible.

Right about now, you are going to want to start meeting people who are outstandingly, surprisingly, and strikingly different from you; people who think and write differently than you do. Even if they seem intolerably strange, intense, and every other unpleasant adjective to you at first, they'll widen your eyes.

One more point before we get into the meat and potatoes: if you and those around you keep going back to the same old subjects again and again, what you write will start to seem stale. Eventually, you'll just start saying the same thing over and over again, and that's one way to get writer's block—and nobody wants that.

The local public library is a surprisingly useful resource. The library itself will probably have a reading series, or may even host occasional discussion groups. At the bare minimum, the staff will have a good sense of who's who and what's going on in the community. Librarians know readers and writers: they make up the library's clientele, after all. Librarians are also usually more than willing to create and set up events that will draw people into the library, so if you and your friends want to do a reading, ask them to provide the space and help with the publicity—both of which they're likely to do at no cost to you.

Furthermore, while you are out on the town meeting all these amazing people, you should be taking advantage of reading in front of them and getting your work out there.

Becka Gregory

Don't watch television. Don't confuse relaxing with vegging out and deactivating your brain. Watching TV is the complete opposite of the relaxation you should be seeking.

Find your writing spot

Find a place that inspires you, a place where you can go to focus on your writing. It doesn't matter where it is or how isolated you need it to be. You know yourself better than anyone else and you know by this point what helps you to get into that writing mood. You need to go out and find that place that sets up the mentality of a writer, as opposed to just writing in a classroom or at your desk, which may leave you with the feeling of being stuck as a student.

Alli Neal

There's a little faerie glen tucked into a mountain in rural Vermont, and I won't tell you where. The Pots is a

> place that was shown to me this past summer. I'm convinced that this place is one of the main contributing factors to the Great Poetry Takeover that hit me last semester. The Pots give me insta-piration, a place where I can go and immediately find myself wanting to write.

Alli Neal's writing spot, the Pots, is her version of the kind of place that every writer should have. It doesn't necessarily have to be somewhere out in the middle of nowhere—a lot of writers work best in coffee shops—and it doesn't even need to be a place where you are all alone. It will provide you with both a haven and an inspiration every time you need to focus. Even if you don't necessarily bust out a ground-breaking poem or a new chapter, it might provide you with the environment necessary to edit a draft, work on character development, or maybe just check a few writer blogs to get some ideas.

Ideally, the classroom will provide you with an environment to bounce ideas back and forth with your classmates and do some workshopping, but you need to find a place of your own beyond the classroom, or you'll never get anything done.

Find a writing process

Every writer is different and we all have different ways of writing. Maybe you like to set an alarm and get up at four in the morning to write. Maybe you keep a notebook on the pillow beside you in case inspiration strikes you in the middle of the night. Maybe you like to listen to your music blaringly loud. Maybe you even have a special playlist just for writing.

The point is that everyone has a writing process. And if you don't, this is the piece of advice that tells you to get one. It will do nothing but help you. Developing a routine or a process or a ritual that goes along with creativity will help you maintain your writing over Thanksgiving break, winter break, the summer, after graduation, and beyond.

For me, I write between breaks in classes. Always. Those two hours between when I get out of work before I have to head to campus? I write. Even if I have nothing interesting on my mind and I don't feel like working on the story that I'm writing at that moment, I write. I write about the uninteresting things that I have on my mind or the unspectacular things that I've encountered that day. I imagine if someone were to ask me to tell them a story, what story I would tell them, and then I write that. I write about what outfit I'm wearing and whom I'm trying to get to notice the outfit that I'm wearing that day. I write imagined conversations that I would have with people who I've never met and will never meet. I write about my ideal date, the perfect wedding, and the type of man I imagine that I'll one day marry. I try to guess what my life is going to be like. I write... well, you get the point.

Build up your writing posse

You never know where you are going to find a good editor, writing partner, idea bouncer-offer, literary sidekick, or whatever else you can think of to call someone who is in your writing posse.

You spent your first year getting to know the people in your classes, other aspiring writers such as yourself, and the people in your res halls. Now it's time to look past the surface a bit. By this point, some people have transferred into the Writing major from other majors. Take those students under your wing. Help them feel welcomed into your writing family. Trust me, by senior year, you'll be drinking wine and talking about your writing together so you might as well start that relationship sooner rather than later.

Then there are the transfer students, for which the same sets of rules apply. These folks have even less of a chance of knowing people since they just arrived on campus, so extend an invitation to a coffee/writing date to them and see what happens.

Now it's all well and good to build bonds with the students you see every day in your classes, but we've already talked about how important it is to look outside of your immediate circle. The students in your classes are learning and experiencing very similar things to you and probably writing about similar things as well. However, someone who is a Criminal Justice major is learning about very different things and probably has different topics to write about than you do. Why not write with them?

Expand outside of the major and see what kind of talent you can find. Even if you find a friend who is an awful, terrible, and horrendous writer, but has excellent stories, you can use them as a resource for gathering material. Why not fictionalize the experiences that you hear from them and create something different than anything you've worked on before?

The best editor I ever had was my grandmother. She was far from a writer; she could barely even write a letter. But boy, could she read. She could sniff out a good story from a mile away and she wasn't shy in telling me that what I was working on sucked or had been beaten to death before. She was one of the most valuable resources that I found when I was first starting out because, unlike all my writing friends, she read like a reader, not like a writer. And my future audience is not going to be all writers, so it was useful to get her input.

There are a lot of people on this earth and you just have to keep your eyes open for the people who are willing and excited to read your work.

Keep building that writing posse.

Work and work-study

It's always tempting to wish you were independently wealthy so you could spend as much time noodling through your novel as you wanted, but (a) most of us are not independently wealthy, (b) most writers are not independently wealthy and (c) being independently wealthy may not actually be good for your writing. Having to get a job, or even several jobs, may well work to your advantage. It all depends on the job and what you make of it.

Some jobs are frankly not very compatible with writing. Any activity that leaves you mentally exhausted, depressed, or anxious kills your writing. Oddly, it's the manual jobs, the ones that leave your mind free to roam and show you an entirely new side of the world, that help you toss all kinds of interesting thoughts into the turbulent pool that is your mind.

Whether on or off campus, a job can offer all kinds of other unexpected benefits. In some cases, it helps to get a job that feeds an already-existing area of interest.

Jillian Towne

This past summer I worked with Spoonful Catering, a catering company out of my hometown that creates all of their dishes using only local and organic ingredients. Working with them, I learned the difference between mesclun and mustard greens, the difference between a lemon brine and a lemon marinade, how foods are prepared differently to accommodate various different food needs and dietary restrictions, and how to relay this information in a way that was easy for the guests to comprehend. These skills will be invaluable to me as a writer; by catering, I've learned a lot of factual information that I would not have retained if I had simply read about it once and then forgot it.

Sometimes, the job may stretch the connection between your interests and what the job asks you to do—but that may not be a bad thing.

Becka Gregory

Earlier in the year, I was rapidly approaching the cutoff date to acquire a work-study job. Needless to say, the pickings were slim in terms of available positions. The only position I was even semi-interested in was for a marketing and promotion intern for the Intervale Center, a sustainable agriculture non-profit. I applied for the job, and was appropriately unsurprised when I received a reply to the tune of "position's been filled."

As I was sorting through the meager amount of job listings on Craigslist, hoping someone would be hiring, I got an e-mail from the Intervale Center. A position had

opened up, although it was in finance, not in marketing and promotion. Even though I knew nothing about
finance, I set up an interview for Friday.

I got the job, securing my work-study award and getting a heap of stress off my shoulders. It's been a little
difficult for a creative minded person like myself to learn
the hard and fast rules of non-profit finance, but I have
also learned more than I ever expected. I am glad that
I accepted what life threw at me, instead of rejecting an
opportunity that has turned out to be awesome.

Any work-study job that involves helping others with their writing also
helps your own writing.

Patience Hurlburt-Lawton

At the end of my freshman year, I began working as a
tutor in the Writing Center. This has been a rewarding
career for me as it approaches the more technical side of
writing. As a creative writer, when I made the decision to
work for the Writing Center last year, it was the moment
I made the commitment to push myself as a writer.
Because I am helping others write, I really have to know
what I am doing, not simply what I am comfortable with.
As a creative writer, it would be very easy for me to just
write poetry and call it a day. However, taking on this job
has seriously improved my technical writing ever since.

Whether you intended to or not, this kind of support work also develops
teaching skills that may be so useful after graduation that they influence
your choice of career.

Start thinking about your goals

Let's face it—when you're 19 or 20 years old, graduation seems like an eternity away. You don't even know what classes you're going to take next semester, so how can you possibly know what you want to do two years from now? But the truth is that graduation isn't that far away and if you don't start planning for it, you are either going to end up like Van Wilder, or be blindsided upon graduation.

Now, let's be clear: I am not telling you that you need to have the next 20 years of your life mapped out or else you are going to fail miserably. In fact, I changed my mind and my interests about 10 times from sophomore to senior year, but I always saw graduation as the finish line and kept that ultimate goal in sight.

What I am saying is that you should have some idea of what you would like to accomplish while you're still in school. Think about the reasons that you're here, and what you are interested in learning. Commit to a goal to learn those things. If you want to write a novel from beginning to end while you still have professors at your fingertips to help you out, then make your goal to write a novel. Be specific.

Just think about how fun it will be to cross off things on your goal list.

I write between breaks in classes.
Always.

Third Year

This is the year when you start reaching out to the world—by traveling, by being actively engaged in the search for your own purpose, your own way of having an impact on readers everywhere.

Erin Gleeson

I was interested in trying something new, so I applied for an internship to work on a segment team at New Hampshire Public Radio. I discovered that I'm highly interested in documentary and creative non-fiction writing with a multi-media aspect. I spoke to authors, scientists, travelers, doctors, cave-diving experts, farmers, a roller-derby team, bonobo researchers, and a robot.

I learned about traditions, festivals, studies, and aid programs. Needless to say, this experience expanded my interests and curiosities, all while developing my writing skills and even improving my vocabulary. Plus, I made some interesting contacts, built my resume, and got a head start on my "real world" experience.

I've realized, however, that this educational/work-related experience is not the only kind of new experience

I should encounter in order to grow as a writer, artist, and person.

So, I decided to pack up this summer and travel. It is my upcoming WWOOF (World-Wide Opportunities on Organic Farms) adventures that will alert my senses and open up whole new worlds to me. I took a French class to prepare, and the class won't only be helpful during travel, but has added a range to my use of language in how I write.

Take charge of your own education

Remember, this is your education, and you're paying for it. Well, your parents may be paying for it, but sooner or later they're going to make you justify the money they're spending!

By now, your education shouldn't be something you suffer through—it should be something you pursue and grab by the throat.

See if you can find a faculty supervisor who's willing to work one-on-one with you so you can do an independent study in an area that interests you both.

Get together a petition to ask for a class that doesn't yet exist. New courses are developed almost entirely on the basis of student demand. Nothing shows student demand better than a list of 20 names, all of whom pledge to take the course if it is developed and offered.

And if a specialized course isn't offered on your campus but is taught at another school nearby, see if you can take it and have the credits transfer.

Ted Horn

When you're in a class, ask yourself: "Am I actually enjoying this? Or is it just something I can see myself trudging into for the rest of my life?"

Explore electives

Your third year is when a broad range of electives becomes available to you—in fact, your college education will probably never be as free and flexible as it is when you're a junior. This is the time to map out the electives you have left and prioritize what you'd like to use them for.

Check out the classes outside of your major available to you and see what interests you.

Yes, you should certainly be taking interesting and challenging writing classes—but if you're interested in photography, graphic design, music, Web design, or marketing, see if there's a course in these areas that looks interesting. If you can make a strong enough case to your advisor that this course will help you grow as a writer, you may well be able to get permission to take it as a writing elective.

Sarah Wheeler

Take as many different creative classes as possible. When you explore any sort of creative field, your overall creativity expands to incorporate fresh ideas. It helps to get outside of the writing world so that you can step outside the box a little bit. That way, when you come back to your keyboard, or pen and paper, you have a new creative outlook. Last year I took Video Storytelling. I had taken so many different writing classes that I thought this would be just another way to improve my writing skills with a fresh outlook. And it worked. At first I fumbled with getting my story into video form and actually getting the equipment to work, but by the end of the semester, I made a great, albeit amateur, video that evoked an emotional response from my class and my teacher. I learned to look at storytelling in a new way, and I've seen it come through in my creative writing since.

Every profession uses writing, and consequently needs writers. Your writing is an important and valued skill, but knowledge of other things may be equally valuable. Take some time to think about the things that you're good at outside of the field of writing, things that you might not have gotten the chance to study yet and would like to.

Think about the classes that you've already taken. Can you combine your writing abilities with something else that you've learned already?

Liz Crawford

The most valuable lessons I have learned have been during classes that I originally thought were going to be easy. In Creative Non-Fiction class we had to write memoirs, and I learned how to dig deeply inside myself to find what was there waiting to come out. In Creative Writing I learned about the art of the story, about the power of words, and about the true nature of poems. Here in Dublin, in Writing in the City, I have learned how to capture a culture with my words and bring it to life for my readers. And it was through Food Writing that I discovered my idea for my Capstone project: I am turning something creative into something professional.

The advice? Just because a class may not be entirely career-driven does not mean it is not important. Everything you have learned can be harnessed, and it all works together, no matter what style of writing you're doing. Do not forego a class simply because you think it won't be beneficial. If it's something you think you would enjoy, take it—you never know what you could learn about your writing and yourself.

Raise your own bar

This may seem like a tall order while you're in the midst of so many changes, but this can (and should) also be the time when you really get a sense of where you're going and kick into a higher gear. You're not just doing what you're told any more. You're doing what you think is important.

Matt Reevy

Be memorable. Go about it however you please, but don't allow people to experience your work and forget who wrote it. Freshman year I wrote a story called "Love Seat," about a furniture fabricator who loves his creations. Literally. And, with the help of a couple other people and some consenting chairs, we performed it at a reading. People still remember that. I've had people I've never met talk to me about it.

Be inseparable from your work. If your writing is worth remembering, then you should be too, and vice versa.

Write things that linger in thoughts on a drunken Sunday afternoon.

Hand out copies of your work on street corners naked in the middle of January.

Compose thank you letters made entirely of literary anachronisms. Whatever you do, make it stick. Because people will remember these things. And people will remember you. And if people remember you, they will read what you write. And that, I suspect, is how you make things happen.

Write beyond campus

One of the most important ways in which you make the switch from being a student writer to being a writer is that you stop thinking of writing as a class assignment. And as soon as you start to think of yourself as writing something that is potentially interesting and even valuable to a reader, well then, you're bound to start thinking of your writing as having a life of some kind out there in the vast world of readers.

Rachel Salois

Over the past year, I have gone from a nice but timid worker to a noisy and shameless self-promoter of my writing. I used to be nervous about asking people to read my blog, let alone convincing people to hire me for their writing internships, but lately I've realized, "Hell, there are a lot of *New York Times* articles and best-selling books that I read and think, 'I could have written that better.'"

The question is not "Who could write something great?" It's "Who is writing something great?" Who has the honest intention of pounding their words over the heads of friends, professors, publishers, and strangers they find in the street until someone actually does read it and realizes, Hey, this is amazing.

If you want to be a better writer, stop thinking of yourself as a student and your class assignments as homework. Think of yourself as a writer and assignments as a way to work towards your larger goals. Make every single thing you write something that is interesting to you and others. The only way to get published is to write like you're already published.

Once you start thinking of yourself as writing for readers, that purpose may well change what you write about, and what genre(s) you choose. There's nothing wrong with this: it doesn't mean your new direction is in any sense less worthy than what you'd been doing before; nor does it mean that everything you've done until now has been a waste of time. You've been developing a range of skills, and now you're expanding that range. Nobody knows what kinds of writing you'll be doing in 10 years' time, but one thing's for certain: it'll draw on all the interests and skills you've acquired over your whole writing life up to that point. What matters is to allow yourself to pursue those interests and develop the necessary skills along the way, continually adding to your abilities as a writer and constantly becoming more interesting as a person.

Jillian Towne

At the end of my sophomore year, I was in full-on poet mode. I had just taken Advanced Poetry, put together a chapbook, and sent off submissions to a dozen different magazines. I wanted to build a cabin in the woods, paint it in a rainbow of colors, buy a dozen journals, and get to it.

Then summer happened, and I spent the entire time cooking, working with clients, and exploring my interests that had very little to do with writing: cooking, traveling, photography, running, hiking. I shucked corn, segmented chickens (admittedly not my favorite task), sold food at a weekly farmers' market, served food at weddings, got lost on a Vermont mountainside, found my stride, and spent a lot of time talking to new people. I came back to school feeling happy and accomplished, though I had barely written a word.

This academic year, I took a very different kind of course load than I have in the past. I haven't taken a single "creative" writing class; everything I have written has had strong roots in reality. I've written less this year than ever before, and I've whined and complained about this several times to several people who are probably very sick of my grumbling at this point. But, my lack of production does not mean that I've been at all removed from the writing world.

I shifted gears substantially, becoming a staff writer and editor for the Champlain College Publishing Initiative. I've worked with clients, helping them complete book projects. And though it has involved a certain amount of hair pulling and swearing and some tears, I've also really enjoyed it.

First semester I edited Ginger Vieira's book *Your Diabetes Science Experiment*. I worked with her and a small team of CCPI staff members, editing the book for content and tone, as well as giving input on design decisions. Working with Ginger was great: I learned how to communicate professionally, how to get over being scared of giving criticism, and how to take myself seriously as a professional editor. It was an immensely valuable experience, one that I recommend to anyone.

Second semester, I ghostwrote a book with Peter Garang Deng, a Sudanese refugee who is using the book as part of a fundraising platform for his own grassroots foundation that sponsors children in Sudan to go to school.

The project was both rewarding and frustrating: to write as if you are someone else is a strange assignment in editing, identity, and letting go of total control. In the end, I learned how to work with a large team on a project, and how incredibly challenging it can be to have too many cooks in the kitchen.

Which brings me back to my summer job. There too I work with clients, and while I love the experience of cooking and arranging and preparing, the real fun of the job is when you get to talk to people about food, local ingredients, and what they like and what they don't.

The same is true with editing and publishing. While I will always create my own work, I've realized that my real passion involves working with clients, helping them to create their own unique vision, offering suggestions and advice, and using any skills I have available (and learning some new ones!) to turn an idea into reality.

Send out your work

By now you've probably already been writing for the campus newspaper or literary magazine, for your own blog, for friends on other campuses—all kinds of outlets. But once again (are you spotting a theme, here?) it's time to broaden your writing horizons and take more risks.

Here's the first, last, and most important point: your real aim is not to get published but to learn more about your writing, and about the business of writing in general.

Why? Well, first of all, the whole thing about being a published writer or not being a published writer is a massive illusion (and possibly a delusion, too).

First off, being published is no guarantee of quality. Haven't you read a hundred pieces of writing published in all sorts of places where you thought, "Jeez, if I can't do better than that I might as well shoot myself now?" Your immediate aim should be a good writer. If that happens, sooner or later you'll be a good published writer.

> *Your immediate aim should be a good writer. If that happens, sooner or later you'll be a good published writer.*

Second, getting hung up on whether or not you've been published is a quick route to (a) writer's block and (b) insanity. All you do is beat yourself up for not being someone who you are not.

Third, stressing over whether a particular poem/story/article/whatever is getting published just takes time away from your time and energy when you could be working on your next poem/story/article/whatever. You have to learn the balance between the necessary time to be spent prospecting (i.e. sending your work out, making follow-up calls or emails, etc.) and the necessary time to be spent writing, and the only way to learn that balance is by trying.

The best way to start this whole phase of your writing career is to think of it like this: you have written something (or, if you're a journalist, you have a story idea) that is, essentially, a ticket. That ticket in itself may turn out to be just a piece of paper, but it gets you in certain doors where you can have certain conversations that will be very, very useful to you. And you can only have those conversations by having a ticket.

So by all means send your work out to big magazines, small magazines, literary periodicals, 'zines, websites, online discussion groups, book agents, book editors, TV and film producers, and do so both humbly and boldly. *Whatever they say, you learn something, and right now learning is your job.* Later your job may be to support a family, but right now you can afford to try and fail.

Even if your work is sent back with a form rejection or no comment at all, you've earned the right to contact that editor (or producer or whatever) and say, "Thanks for taking the time to look at my work. It's not what you are looking for, and that's fine. But if you wouldn't mind, I'd like to ask you for five more minutes of your time. Can you please give me one suggestion, as someone who is just starting out as a writer, how I could improve?"

By releasing that person from the obligation of having to buy your work, you turn yourself, in a sense, into his or her *protégé*—and the French word protégé means "protected." Seven out of 10 editors (or whatever) will think, "S/he's just a kid, s/he's just starting out, why not give him/her the benefit of my wisdom?" And that's what you're after, right now.

So much of the process of sending out your work is about getting used to the process, learning the landscape.

It changes you as a person. Someone who does good work in class is still a writing student. Sooner or later you have to come to terms with the fact that nobody is going to come looking for your good work—you have to go out in search of people who might be interested in it.

Emotionally, that's a huge change. You're bound to go through a phase when you think you're an imposter, that people are going to see your writing and just crack up, or dump all over it. Even once you've started to discover that rarely happens, you still need to work out what kinds of places (Newspapers? Magazines? Websites? Radio stations?) are most receptive to what you're trying to do.

And somewhere in that process you start getting more professional about how you present your work and yourself, how to describe what you do, what its value is, even how you talk over the phone or by email. Even (gasp!) how you dress.

Enter writing contests

Writing contests may sound like the shortcut to fame and fortune, and also a chance to assess just how good you're getting as a writer, but be aware of two things:

* **Most writing contests are created as publicity and marketing tactics.** It may look as though the magazine or organization has created the contest in order to encourage, discover and reward new talent, but they've probably done it to raise their own profile and attract a raft of new material that is essentially donated to them. Some contests even act as fund-raisers: the prize for the winning entry/entries is usually only a fraction of the admission fees. So in other words, don't expect a writing contest to lead to fame and fortune.

  More importantly, don't let writing contests and literary magazines convince you what you should be writing. The contest is to help them get what they want, not to help you get what you want.

* **Most writing contests are a bit of a lottery.** Anyone who has judged one of these contests knows that so many submissions come in there's just not enough time to read every one carefully. And if the judging is carried out by a panel, the judges often disagree wildly over their personal favorites. In other words, don't mistake a writing contest for an accurate and professional assessment of your ability as a writer.

Does this mean you shouldn't enter writing contests? Not necessarily. First of all, entering a contest makes you feel like a writer, and frankly that's a feeling worth cultivating, especially if it makes you put all that extra effort into making your submission look professional, making sure you've got the address right, and even making sure you've learned a little about the publication or organization. These are all part of the great project of learning about the writing profession and how to flourish in it.

Second, it's just possible that you may be able to learn something about your writing by entering the contest. As we say, the judges are usually far too swamped to be able to comment on (or even remember!) most of the entries, but if you contact them after the dust has settled and jog their memories a little, they may be able to offer a little feedback.

The point is, winning writing contests isn't everything. The judge of a writing contest is not God; nor is the editor of the *New Yorker*. In the end, you should aim be a tougher, fairer judge of your own work than anyone else. Other people's opinions serve mainly to help you learn how to form your own opinion of your writing.

Ted Horn

A friend of mine told me about a writing contest held by a company called the Black Library. They deal with science fiction, which is a genre I have read, just not in bulk. "I'll just write about futuristic stuff," I thought.

As I read on, however, I found out that this competition would confine participating writers to the limits of the company's own fictional universe. I read some previously submitted and selected pieces in the archives and felt okay—competitive, even. I've never been given all the details, and this competition did just that. The planets, galaxies, types of clothing, building styles, rankings, titles, species (it is science fiction, after all) and every other little thing. I was given several chances for, let's say, personal customization for my submission because this was a surprisingly developed world.

This was a new dynamic and I spent a lot of time researching and trying to compile everything into a coherent story. Unfortunately, I didn't make it past round one. However, I did write about 16 satisfying pages and 47 pages of "okay" writing.

I met rejection again, and that's always valuable to a

writer. More importantly, I learned a little bit about having deadlines. I learned a lot about researching what's important and, in an almost journalistic sense, felt a little more educated in my ability to pick out what's interesting and gripping, rather than what will just fill a page.

Think about an internship

Although most students do internships in their senior year or even after they graduate, there's nothing wrong (and a whole lot right) with doing more than one internship. It's not just about developing job skills: it's amazing how much the simple act of getting out of the house and off campus can open your eyes.

You can never start to plan too early. So, what area would you like to work in? An internship doesn't necessarily mean that you are going to start your career in that field after you graduate, but it could also be a good way to get your foot in the door at a place that you might want to pursue a job at. So try to find something that you might be interested in long-term.

Now start thinking about specific skills (writing and otherwise) you'll need to have in order to land that internship and not fail miserably. Do you already have those skills? If not, what classes do you need to take in order to get them? And if you don't know what skills you'll need, who do you need to talk to in order to find out? The sooner you get the ball rolling, the easier it's going to be for you to find that internship.

Once you have the skills you'll need to acquire between then and now under control, you need to start networking. Who do you need to be in contact with in order to put yourself on the radar? The Career Services department at your school is a good place to start, but they can only help you so much. You have to take responsibility for finding your internship into your own hands. It's your job to make sure that you've got one secured for yourself.

You can also contact the professor who is responsible for the internship class and see what internships people have really enjoyed doing in the past and gotten a lot out of. Or, you could take the whole thing into your own hands and propose something that's never been done before. If you have a specific field of interest that's a little outside of the box, you should look into places nearby and contact them and the professor in charge of the internships and see if you can work something out.

Kayleigh Blanchette

For the past year I've been interning for *Vermont Commons*. The editor has thrown two vox populi interview assignments my way so far, and I gained a lot of experience from each. My second interview was with Charlotte Dennett, a candidate for the progressive party in Vermont who wrote a book about the prosecution of George W. Bush. This interview was very rewarding because I independently met with her, interviewed, recorded, transcribed, composed an article, edited it, and turned it in within a three-week period. The experience has been incredibly helpful in my writing. And since Dennett used to be a journalist, she gave me tips on interviewing, which I also took away. For example, in Ethnographic Writing, I already had interviewing and transcribing experience while most of my classmates didn't. Getting published is a perk as well.

Develop your Web presence

It's time to think beyond blogging or creating a simple online portfolio and to ask yourself how the Web can work for you.

You should develop your Web presence for at least three good reasons: one, it's fun. Two, whatever kind of writer you are, it gets you thinking actively about finding and developing a readership. And three, it teaches you a set of skills that employers want very, very badly. An employer advertising for a writer these days may well assume that you have good Web and social media skills, and may not hire you if you don't, no matter how good of a writer you are.

The first step is to move beyond a basic blog site. You want to create something that looks less generic, and you also want to learn how to take the face off the clock, so to speak, and tinker around with the works. Spending $10 a year for your own domain name and $7 or so per month for Web hosting won't break you—and in fact your parents might well pay for it, as it'll be a sign you're taking your professional future seriously and perhaps their tuition money won't have been wasted after all.

You can create a site full of original material. Poems, essays, stories, photos, screenplays, video—the trick here is to find a strong sense of coherence and to answer the question "What makes my work stand out?" Rachel Salois' site younghipsexyactivism is an editorial site supported with excellent architecture, striking art and a clear point of view. If you check out Clara Barnhart's site (ClaraBarnhart.wordpress.com), you'll find not only text, but audio versions of some of her poetry, like you'd find on a band site—that's not only cool and personal but really unusual.

Becka Gregory

I actually got a request to do a beer review by a Switchback employee at Finnegan's last night!

You can create a content-aggregation site. This is where you choose a topic that interests you and create a site that pulls material you like off the Web like a "Best Of" anthology. Ted Horn and Kayleigh Blanchette created a comedy site called Go For The Jocular that was well-designed, attractive, and full of surprises. Matt Reevy discovered that if he set up a music site, bands would send him all kinds of recordings, home video, and band news. As long as you don't violate copyright, this can be a whole lot of fun—and in most cases the people whose work you're re-posting are glad of the exposure.

Matt Reevy

My site snagged another 192 visits from 152 people this week. And it's all thanks to the Domino Effect. The first band I featured are pretty low-key. 60 Facebook fans, no Myspace. Not a whole lot of online presence. The limited presence they do have, though, brought me the second band, who saw that entry and wanted one. They have 200-ish Facebook fans. Through them, the third band (who I'm putting up this evening) got in touch with me. They have 2000-ish Facebook fans. I don't do math, but the audience has grown accordingly—and my paean to all things slow and loud spreads its tentacles ever-farther into the Internet sonicsphere.

You can combine the two. As a sophomore, Molly McGlew began her blog, Vixxxen, as a content aggregator, combining her interests in snowboarding, art, and fashion, but she also added video footage and still photos from her own trips to the slopes. The result has become so successful that several snowboard apparel companies now sponsor her.

Next, you need to learn how to drive traffic (or, as we say in the writing biz, attract readers) to your site.

Make sure you've got Google Analytics or WordPress Stats or some other kind of tracker installed. This not only helps you see how many people have visited your site, more importantly it shows you where they've come from, it tells you a little about why they might have checked you out, and in many instances it gives you a way of turning the Web around and getting in touch with them.

Let's start simple. You want to know how many people have visited your site because it allows you to experiment with your site and see what kinds of response you get. Remember, there are no hard and fast answers with the Web: we're all figuring it out as we go along. Should you use a lot of splashy color? A music track? Embedded video? Should you tie in your Facebook and Twitter feeds? What works well on one site is death on another. So you want to see yourself as constantly building your site, trying new content, new approaches, and tracking stats to see what gets the best response.

Why did they visit, and how did they find you? Again, you want to know the answers to these questions because it helps tell you what you're doing right. What browser searches did they do to find you? What tags seem to have attracted attention?

Now turn it all around. If someone came to you from another site, check out that site to see what sent the visitor to you. If someone else has written about your site, thank them. Offer to trade links. Start building a constructive online relationship or collaboration.

If possible, get in touch with the visitor. Remember, this may seem like a casual online surfing encounter or just a statistic, but if you were in a bookstore or a library giving a reading and someone came to hear you, you'd want to build on that brief encounter and at least exchange a few words. It may amount to nothing—and often does—but it may open all kinds of doors, personal and professional.

Constantly think about creating and then expanding your network. Use social media. Join online groups dedicated to your area of interest, post questions to them, join discussions, strike up online friendships.

Jillian Towne

I made several attempts to boost my site views this week—and they worked! I wrote two new blog posts, announcing each one to my Facebook friends. I also posted a new piece of prose, which I announced as well. I gave LinkedIn another shot, which went much better than last week; while I didn't receive any comments from those folks yet, my Site Stats reader tells me that most of my views today (over 70!) came from the LinkedIn community. Finally, I reached out personally to people in my network who aren't avid Facebook users, which got me some additional hits. Oh, and I shamelessly "liked" my site on StumbleUpon (which I highly recommend doing. Really. Go do it. I'll wait).

Pulitzer or Bust

At first it may seem as if this is pushy: why would these strangers be interested in you, your thinking, your writing? After a while, though, you will probably discover that online readers can be incredibly generous and supportive. You barely even realize it while it happens, but after some time it hits you: you are a writer with readers. Your work is being read. You are out there in the world.

Erin Gleeson

Since the changes and updates I've received some very kind comments from both LinkedIn members, CouchSurfers and from some friends. One flattering comment was that my poetry was good enough to eat! (What a confidence boost.)

This week's visits are at 58, with 287 page views, averaging at 8:31 minutes per view.

Get the heck out of Dodge

Junior year is the perfect time to travel. You're feeling more self-sufficient and adult, yet you don't have to worry about job-hunting just yet. Besides, by now the campus is getting to be so familiar you really need a jolt of something new, exciting, and different.

Ashley DeFelice

Going to Ireland was a bit of a risk, though I brilliantly didn't realize it until I got there. I remember getting to my apartment with my bags, no Internet connection, no roommates (not that day, at least), and a fever (naturally), and just panicking because I felt so lost and there was no one around to talk to. But since then, I've adored it here. I've found new things to write about, and I've done things that I never would have done at home. Like purposely planning out a solo spring break trip to Cork. I planned out my bus ride and my hostel by myself. And then I planned nothing else, so I could be free. I planned to figure it out all by myself. And I did! And I wrote about it. And then I broke my camera on the first day—honestly, I could write so much on what has gone wrong since I got to Ireland, but I don't regret it—so instead of crying, I wrote down everything I saw in my journal. I took bus trips and train rides to Blarney Castle, Kinsale, and Cobh, and in all of those places I wrote. I made myself capture everything—the bright green of the grass, the specific sweetness of the air, the way the rows of houses weaved in and out like waves.

Any kind of travel will do. Road trip, Alternative Spring Break, study abroad, epic hitchhiking adventure—every kind of travel opens your eyes and makes you question your assumptions, but for a writer travel provides a constant flow (or sometimes avalanche) of new material. It's exactly the opposite of high school writing class, when the teacher came in and gave you a writing prompt, forcing you to write about something that you were at best half-interested in. When you travel, life itself is throwing prompts at you from every direction, and it would be harder not to write.

All this new material may also give you a new sense of direction, both in your life and in your writing.

Abbie Clark

This whole year has been a learning experience for me, in the sense that I have become even more independent than I already was and learned what I want to do in life. Most of my self discovery was caused by other people who made me realize what happiness is, and that even though I like to please everybody sometimes I need to take a break and do what I feel is right, but the biggest part of my self discovery was my drive to stick to my Bucket List.

I started keeping a bucket list when I was in high school, and I have been constantly adding to it over the years. Some of the stuff on my bucket list revolved around China, and when I went to a study abroad fair in October and saw a faculty member passing out fliers for a class that would travel to China, I didn't back down. Once I set my heart to it I made it happen. Being a sophomore, I had to make sure I could get credit as a writing elective. Once in China all I wanted to do was experience it.

Since getting back, my travel bug bite has gotten bigger and I realized that what I want to do is travel writing. Before China I didn't really have a focus in the writing major. I love writing poetry, enjoyed creative non-fiction, and realized I liked journalism. Now, I've decided to start blogging more about my travels and completing my bucket list. I talked with the current editor-in-chief of the campus newspaper about having a travel writing column. It will be an editorial style, discussing the adventure there with a little historic background. I'm wicked excited about it, and I feel if someone has a goal like my bucket list then don't give it up, no matter what people tell you.

Think about new directions

Your junior year may also be the time when this spreading-your-wings phase leads you to change your focus—the focus of your writing, or the focus of your life, or both. You venture far enough outside your comfort zone to discover that some of the things you took for granted might be worth questioning, or even changing.

Matthew Forrest

Writing isn't everything. There is a reason horses wear blinders and humans don't. I myself have tried many different things: banking, modeling, sailing, farming, cooking, teaching; they were all interesting, and they all taught me something valuable that, had I been stuck on becoming a writer, I would never have learned. I love writing; I know that for a fact. But the only reason I know that is because I have tried everything else. How can you know you're supposed to be a writer if all you ever do is try to become a writer? How do you know you're not supposed to be a fisherman? You never know until you try.

Don't choose a path; that never works. Find your path. Only then can you be sure you're where you belong. You need to experience everything life has to offer, otherwise you will be constantly living in doubt. And while writing may beget writing, doubt always begets misery.

This may be scary, and you may interpret it as a sign that you've somehow messed up, but don't worry. You still have a year or more of college left to make those changes and adjustments and still graduate with your feet on the ground.

There's also a vital lesson here for you as a writer. A writer's life involves a whole lot of discoveries and changes of direction. The great part is, you're the one who's in charge of deciding where your life takes you next. Of course, the hard part is, you're the one who's in charge of deciding where your life takes you next. It's best to see this as a good thing!

Paul Oka

In my third year, I was academically dismissed because of my poor grades and general lack of motivation. This was entirely my fault and what I consider to be "hitting rock bottom." So I went to the community college for a year. This was a really good learning experience for me. My time at the community college made me realize the importance of a higher education and how seriously I had squandered my parents' resources. A lot of my classmates were blue-collar workers whose bodies quit on them or single mothers. It took me having to witness what I would become if I put off getting an education to really motivate me.

You only ever improve as a writer by taking risks. At first you tried something new with a sentence, or a paragraph. By now, though, you're starting to take risks with how you live your life.

Ashley DeFelice

I don't regret the things I do nearly as much as I regret the things I don't. The night last month I went out and had my coat, Massachusetts ID, and 12 euro stolen? Well, I wish I still had those things, but I'm still glad I went out. It makes a good story, anyway. But the nights I did nothing, just sat with my roommates and watched TV? Some of those I do regret, because you can do that sort of thing anywhere. I want to make my life interesting. It's the best way to become an interesting writer.

Be a trend

And no, we're not talking about fashion here. I'm sure you've all heard the expression "Be the change you want to see in the world?" Well, the same general principle applies for making a spot for yourself in the writing world. If you want to stand out against your competition, you need to make sure that you stand out among your competition. The best way to do that is to show how different, and unique, you are from everyone else.

If you've ever read one of the dull, paint-by-numbers books on writing that your professors just love to make you read, and thought to yourself, I could do it better than them, then do just that. Do something that is going to set you apart, and maybe even inspire others to follow your lead. Create a change in your writing that is going to sky rocket you into opportunities. It's possible you may even want to create a change in your image, as well, whether it be how your online image comes across to the viewer, or your level of professionalism, or your cover letter skills.

Whatever it is you choose to do, you want to be a trend, not a follower. And you want to be a trend that others will want to follow.

Fourth Year

Now you've mastered all the basics of writing and started thinking independently of your classes, it's time to start acting independently of your classes. This means when people ask you what you do, you don't say "I'm a writing major" but "I'm a writer." And you start taking initiative for your future life, and that long, meandering exploration called a writer's career. Welcome to senior year, the beginning of the end. Or maybe the end of the beginning.

Eric Voorhis

During senior year I think it's important to focus on one aspect of writing. Writing majors cover a lot of territory and many different styles, which is one of the things that drew me in. But toward the end I would recommend you zero in on the type of writing you're most passionate about, whether it's fiction or journalism, grant writing or screenwriting.

Avoid senioritis

I am a senior. At some point (hopefully) we'll all be seniors.

And let me tell you, once you reach senior year, you're only here to get that diploma. Unless you want to go on to even higher education and enter into an MFA program, you are over school. You are done with professors and their silly assignments, and you don't care about the college anymore. You have better things to do than homework and essays. You just want to be done. Am I getting warm?

Well, you can want to be done all you want to, but the fact is that you aren't done. You have two semesters left before you get that diploma and are free to do whatever you like. Instead of being miserable for the next eight months, you should try to make the best of the situation. Try your damnedest to enjoy your last year because I've heard from graduates that you're really going to miss it when it's over.

So try to stay on top of your game, because you're soon going to need all the game you've got. Here are some tips to designing your education that I've compiled to help you avoid the dreaded senioritis.

Capstone project/whatever

These are all variations on the same name and it doesn't matter what your school calls it. I'll say Capstone because that's what it is at my school, but you can refer to it however you see fit. What the Capstone comes down to is the culmination of your college life. This is the final paper, this is the final project. This is what you have been preparing to do for three years and now here it is. And you have some decisions to make.

First and most importantly, what is it about you and your work that you would like to showcase in your Capstone? What topics interest you? I don't know the specific requirements of your senior project or independent study, but you should so take a moment (or several) to think about it. And think about something that really, really interests you, not something that you think will help you get an A, or something that fits the requirements of your school's project.

This needs to be something that you want to spend a semester working on. And not the same amount of work that you pay to your other classes, but an almost immeasurable amount of time working on: researching, writing, editing, rewriting, re-editing, more writing, more editing, and so forth. You are going to be practically married to this thing, so you are going to want to take a while to think about what to do. And instead of letting it freak you out like my previous sentence may have, think about it as the ultimate opportunity. You get to choose your topic. This may be the first time that you have been given such freedom—and so much time to develop your work into something really substantial. Instead of letting that hold you back, take advantage of it. Choose a great topic and rock it.

> This may be the first time that you have been given such freedom—and so much time to develop your work into something really substantial.

Independent studies are a little different because they aren't as much a requirement of the school as an example of one of the ways that you can take control over your own education. In order to obtain an independent study, you need to have a specific project to work on in mind and a goal for the semester. If you want to write a novel, you write a proposal for your novel and create a timeline for the semester. And after you have your project picked out, you need to find a faculty member that will be in charge of your independent study.

An independent study is only going to work for you if you are willing to dedicate yourself to the project. You can't get sick of it and throw it away with the garbage like some of the work you produced in your first few years. If nothing else, it would be a good practice in commitment. But it could really help you fight off those anxious feelings that come along with being a senior and help you avoid getting bored with the semester and tired of all your classes.

One more point, and it's one of those good news/bad news things. An independent study will also free you up from the tedium of going to class at the same times every week. That's the good news. The bad news is that you'll have to start managing your own time, which, trust me, is a lot harder than you think it will be. Better to start figuring that out now, though, than in 12 months' time....

Electives, electives, electives

Do you remember sophomore year when you started to pick the classes that you wanted to take? Well now it's senior year and hopefully you left yourself some electives to play around with. (General electives would be especially nice at this point.) Electives are going to help you to avoid senioritis because they are going to ensure that you take some of the classes that interest you instead of only the ones that are required to get your diploma.

You don't want to graduate with any regrets about classes you might have taken.

Think about it this way: do you really want to spend your last year stuck in classes with a bunch of people who are forced to be in those classes?

It's bad enough that there are certain classes you have to take, but it's even worse when you have to take them in your last year, or last semester. Trust me: if you didn't want to take some required course as a sophomore, you are going to want to take it even less as a senior.

In my case, I barely wanted to take electives, but it has made senior year a lot more bearable to be able to choose the classes that I want to take.

At least I have some vague interest in the courses that I'm enrolled in rather than being stuck listening to professors prattle on and on about subjects that I couldn't care less about. I even saved the class I've been the most excited to take for my final semester as a reward for making it so far.

So, trust me on this one: you are going to want electives for your senior year. And general electives are like pure gold. If for the time being you've been doing so much writing you're temporarily sick of it—trust me, it happens—you can use those golden electives to take any class that you want. Peruse the list of classes available and pick something wild. I used up all of my general electives when I changed majors, but if you have any left, take advantage of them. It's senior year—you've earned it.

Alli Arbuthnot

Don't rush. You're graduating! Savor it. If you can, try to avoid packing up your Subaru and taking your final drive down Main Street the day after the ceremony. Chill. Have a cup of coffee with your favorite professor or mentor.

You will miss these simple things will all your heart, and although you'll visit, it's never going to be the same again. Adulthood isn't going anywhere, and this is your summer. Rock on.

Bend the rules

The program you're in was created to help you to become the best writer that you can be, and to expose you to a wide variety of writing alleys that you want to go down. But like almost everything else in life, it's not perfect. Nothing that's been designed to accommodate a large group of people with a variety of different learning needs is going to be perfect for everyone. Only you know what works for you and what you are really looking for in your education.

We've all heard the old cliché that rules were meant to be broken, or at the very least, bent a little bit, so go for it. Why not try to make some of those general electives a part of your writing curriculum?

If there is a series of classes that you want to take (say in website development, for example), approach the program director or department chair at your school about it and see how they can help you fit those classes into your schedule without putting you behind schedule to graduate.

It can never hurt to ask, and if your faculty care about their students and their students' education, they will take the time to at least consider letting you take the class. But you have got to be willing to make your case. You have got to want it and be willing to fight for it. They won't let you count Intermediate Photography as a writing elective without some explanation as to how exactly it's going to help you become a better writer.

You don't want to graduate with any regrets about classes you should have taken when you had the opportunity and you don't want to waste your time sitting through Screenwriting if you aren't interested in it and would rather be taking something else. This is your last year, so make it all it can be.

Now you've got a handle on how to design your education so as to avoid crawling up the walls during your final year, it's time to move on to other little things that could help you make it to graduation in May.

Be your own toughest critic

You're getting to the point where how well you write and how hard you work are no longer defined by the course or the professor: they're defined by you. You're on the threshold of having to make those decisions for the rest of your life, so by now you'd better know what you're capable of, and how to get the most out of yourself. You'd better practice doing really, really good writing, because after this year it isn't practice any longer. It's the real thing.

Julia Grunewald

Write for an audience scarier than your professor.

By this point, you've been writing long enough to know that you've mastered the basics. You know how to use semicolons and you can articulate an argument well. This sounds like a great thing, but in some ways it's actually harmful to your advancement as a writer.

If you go to a small school, you probably have had all your senior year teachers before. You know which ones will love the paper you write the morning it's due and which ones you need to pull two all-nighters just to get a B.

This is how I was at the beginning of this year. If I wanted to, I could have done quite well without really developing my writing past the point it was at a year ago. Well, I could have, except I decided to take a class in grant writing.

For this course, I needed to work with a non-profit in the community as their grant writer. I'd never written (or even read) a grant before January, and I had no idea how I was expected to write something I knew practically nothing about for an organization that did this all the time. It was terrifying. Terrifying, but it made me a better writer.

Because I was so uncomfortable with the medium, and because I was giving it to an organization and not a professor, I put many hours into each two page document. I made sure that the words I used were exactly the ones I was going for, and I spent a long time analyzing my tone to make absolutely sure it couldn't be misconstrued.

Subconsciously, I took this attention to detail with me in everything I wrote this semester, and produced much better papers than I could have otherwise.

So if you really want to improve your writing in your senior year, find a creative way to challenge yourself.

Make the most of internships

We talked at length about how to land your internship and how important it is to find an internship that's interesting to you, but now you are actually out in the field completing it, and you're probably thinking that you are in way over your head. (I know that's what I thought, at least.) So what do you do now that you're out there doing it for real?

Jacquelene Adams

The most important thing you can do before graduating is intern and take the internship seriously. Your internship is the key into the industry of your choice. It will open doors to new connections, networking, and great experience. Treat your internship like you would a serious job: seriously. Your internship will probably be the first job on your resume that is relevant to the career you want to have, so making a good impression, working harder than you ever have, and going above and beyond expectations is very important. It is very hard, if not impossible, to land a job without prior experience in the industry.

An internship is unlike anything else you've done during your time in college. You may have gotten away with pulling all-nighters to finish your assignments for class, but you won't have the same success continuing that pattern with your internship. While you pay money to attend classes, the only person you are hurting by not paying attention is yourself. A worthwhile internship involves work that will affect multiple people if you don't complete the part you are responsible for, so all of a sudden other people are depending on you, which changes everything. Not to mention that if you don't pull your weight you may get fired.

On the other hand, you don't want to let that responsibility get to you to the point where you scream, throw up your hands and run for the hills. Remember: every intern is in the same boat, thinking they have no idea what they're doing and feeling like a complete fraud.

Doug Tetrault

From the moment I arrived in Washington, D.C., I realized that I wasn't in Kansas anymore, and I was never going to be the same.

My first basic fear was that my education and interest in American government and politics would be inadequate and not allow me to compete at the level I would need to. I knew Washington would be full of extremely gifted young people; students who had studied political science, economics, law, and international relations. That can be very intimidating.

My second fear was more personal. I was traveling half way across the country with no support, no money, and no idea where I was going. I was scared I would get lost and not be able to find where I was going to live, where I was going to work, and where I could buy basic things like groceries. Overcoming those fears and just "doing it" made the experience what it was.

The internship was an incredible experience, but it did have some downsides. First off, while I was exposed to some of the most important hearings of the year and met and spoke with some of the most incredible and influential public servants in government, I was also just an intern. I made copies, set up hearing rooms, acted as a door person, etc. I was able to get my hands on some research projects, but a lot of the internship had to do with light administrative work. It was up to me to actively pursue more challenging assignments—which I did—but that was not the main purpose of the program.

The advice I'd offer? Be yourself, but understand that no one cares who you are until you prove you're worth caring about. If you don't go to Washington, but some other crazy place—never let an opportunity pass; you will regret it. Be willing to do anything they ask. Be open to new people. Tell them you want to learn and that you want them to give you the resources to do so, whether it be legislative briefs, websites, conference invitations, or just plain old human discussion.

Don't let your geographic or current situation hold you back. I left a steady girlfriend with no money in my pocket and moved to the most intimidating political city in the country to intern for the most powerful committee in the Senate and I would never take it back. It was hard; it was lonely, and I came home with less than $30 to my name; but it was worth all the trouble and the experience is probably why I had a full-time job that I wanted to have, by the end of the summer. Internships—like life—are what you make of them.

It may seem to you that the key part is landing the internship (and the second key part is surviving!), but anyone who has had a successful internship has told me that it all comes down to what you make of it as an opportunity. It must be strange to arrive in a totally unfamiliar place as the youngest and most inexperienced person there and think of yourself as being the one who will make things happen (for you, at least), but it seems to be true. If you carry on thinking of yourself as a nobody or a doormat, that's how people will treat you. If you can manage to think of yourself as someone who is there to make a contribution, no matter how small, and to get something out of the experience for yourself, then you may surprise yourself by what initiatives you take, and what you get out of them.

Alex Tirpack, who describes himself as "the son of a dentist from New

Jersey," found himself in the internship program at *Rolling Stone* surrounded by the kids of celebrities. On their first day, all the interns were told never to imagine they'd ever write anything for the magazine, and sure enough, the assignments were pretty basic.

"I was a regular old editorial intern," Alex explained. "They ask you to work at least three days a week from 10 a.m. until 6 p.m. When I first started, I worked four days a week. Every morning the interns go through the day's newspapers, clipping any articles the editors and writers would be interested in. We would make a news packet from the articles, make a million copies, and then distribute the packet to the editors and writers. This had to be done before noon. Other typical intern duties included researching various subjects for writers and editors, transcribing interviews, and yes, running errands."

Through a combination of initiative and just plain getting bored doing these undemanding jobs, Alex looked around for something better, even if it meant working longer hours with no guarantee of any kind of reward.

"Eventually, I took on bigger and more important projects. This took more time and effort, but it was also much more rewarding. I became close with my editor/writer, Austin Scaggs, writing little bits and pieces for his column in the magazine, and interviewing people."

This is the kind of dedication that internship supervisors are looking for. If you've chosen your internship well, it may just turn into something more.

"When my summer internship was over, he asked me to stay and help him start a new blog. So for the next eight months I wrote the 'Smoking Section' blog, five days a week. Ghostwriting is a better term since my name was hardly printed, but it was still some of the most impressive writing I've done. Some days I wrote nearly a dozen posts. I've interviewed people like Paige McConnell, George Clinton, Ben Folds, Dean Ween, and others. I haven't paid for a concert in months. I've booked bands for live in-office performances. It was a great experience."

Even if your internship doesn't turn into a job, bear in mind that the evaluation or recommendation you get from your internship supervisor is probably one of the most valuable boosts you'll get in your job search.

Employers like hearing from your teachers and program director, but they are especially interested to hear how you did in the workplace. So make sure you get your supervisor to write something about you—and it doesn't hurt to have made a good impression!

Start your job hunt early

Graduation is probably the scariest thing I've ever had to consider. I'm a senior. I am only one semester away from finally being released into the "real world" after being a student for 16 years. I've never been more scared in my life. Where am I going to live? Where am I going to work? How am I going to make money in order to afford paying the bills? What's my plan for finding a place to live and a job? Does everyone else have a plan? Why don't I have a plan?

It's enough to give me a panic attack just thinking about thinking about

Finding a job and starting a career are all about connections.

my future. Like it or not, ready or not, in five months the president of this college is going to hand me a diploma that I don't know what to do with. Something that should be the biggest accomplishment and the biggest happiness in my young life is the biggest source of stress and anxiety.

So take a deep breath with me. Inhale deeply and let it out slowly. Take a couple of them if you need it. Thinking about your future is important, but it's not worth having a heart attack over. Don't overwhelm yourself. If you need to take it one day at a time and see where you are at the end of each day, then take it one day at a time. That's probably a better tactic to use than trying to apply for 10 jobs in one day and end up half-assing all 10 in order to get them all done. Take as much time as you need to prepare yourself mentally, but just recognize that it's going to take time, and that you'll need to start the hunt early.

Finding a job and starting a career is all about connections. At this point you should have already made a fair number of professional connections through building an online presence and attending conferences and getting involved in things outside of the classroom and off campus. But now it's time to take advantage of those contacts and see how they could lead you to a job that will actually pay you for your writing. Using an example from my own life, my best friend's mother is a headhunter. She gets people jobs for a living. So it would have been very naïve of me not to ask her for help and advice on how to land a career and not just a job.

You may not have the same types of connections as I do, and that's fine. Everyone is different. It's all about gaining the information that you need to have before you need to have it. Do you know where the best places to look for jobs are? Do you know the best ways to go about applying for a job? How about interviewing techniques and skills? These are all things that you're going to need to know when you start looking. The earlier you know them, the better.

Jacquelene Adam

Cold-email editors. If you are looking for a job in the magazine industry, grab a few magazines that you would like to work for and turn to the masthead. These people are your way in: email them. They may have emails listed in the masthead and if not, search online. It is possible to find editors' emails—you just have to take some time to search. Email managing editors, senior editors, and associate editors. Explain that you are a recent graduate and how much you would love the opportunity to meet with them to discuss how you can break into the industry. You may only hear back from one person, but that is one more connection that you did not have before.

You want to start your job hunt early because (and I hate to explain it this way to college seniors about to graduate!) this is the next phase of your education. You have learned all kinds of writing skills over the past four years or so, but you have barely begun to learn the ins and outs of the writing profession, or of any profession, for that matter. Yep: it's yet another learning curve.

And what we all know about learning curves by now is that you learn by making mistakes. So better start making those mistakes sooner rather than later.

There's another important reason to start the job hunt early, though: money. Not as in "How much?" but as in "When?"

If there's one skill I pride myself on, it's that I'm a researcher. I started looking into how the job-hiring process works from the employer's point of view—always a good thing to know—and this is what I found.

* When an employer has a position that needs filling, he or she (let's say "she" just to keep things simpler) writes up a job description and advertises it, which is when you first see the job posting. You brush up your resume and fine-tune your cover letter and shoot them off with your fingers crossed.

* You probably won't hear anything, except maybe a confirmation that your application has been received, for anything from two to five weeks. The employer is hoping to get a strong pool of applicants, and then take another few days, even a week or more, to pick the most likely candidates and set up interviews.

* The interview process may all be done in one round, which can take another two to four weeks, or it may well involve two rounds, in which case the job offer may well not be made until as long as three months from the time you first applied.

* Even if you are offered the job and you accept, the start date may well be another few weeks, even a couple of months, from the date when you are officially hired.

* Oh, and you were counting on this paycheck to help cover your moving costs and your first month's rent, plus damage deposit, weren't you? Bad news: your first paycheck might not show up until a week or even a month after you start work.

Counting backwards, then, if you want some cash in hand by, say, the September after you graduate, you'd better start applying around winter break after the first semester of your senior year. That's a semester before you graduate. You barely know what classes you're going to be taking, you may even change up your schedule before classes begin again. But you should be applying for a job that could start your career. No pressure or anything.

What's going to happen if you don't listen to this advice and apply early? Well, for me, it would look a lot like me working at Kmart as a college graduate, which isn't the future that I want. It could look like unemployment or a dead-end job that you'll probably get stuck doing for about three years longer than you had planned to do it. Nothing good comes from procrastination.

It's all about initiative.

Claire Bennet

I think my degree program prepared me for life after college as well as it could. My advice from teachers was helpful, even if it did flatten me sometimes. A lot of the classes were really useful in terms of down-to-earth, practical advice about the nitty gritty in real life. The career office advisor's lecture component on the internship requirement was also extremely helpful. She gave a lot of really invaluable advice about networking, preparing for interviews, and the like. When I started really job hunting, I felt like I was prepared to market myself well, and to interview well.

Put down this book and start your search, even if it's just a general one to see what's out there. Now. Go get your feet wet.

Build your network of professionals

Writing can feel very solitary, especially if you are unpublished. Many young writers fill their days with writing, rewriting, and waiting for the next rejection slip, only to have the process start all over again. At best, you might get feedback from a critique group you've formed in your spare time or read about publishing news on an Internet posting you follow. This is one of the reasons why it is so important for writers (especially new writers) to get away from their computers and meet other writers, especially writers in your own field, especially writers who are making a living, or part of a living, at their craft.

One of the most useful things you can do is go to writing conferences. Typically you'll be able to find two or three within driving distance during your final year (look for a state writers' association or a local chapter of the National Writers Union), and they are a great opportunity to meet and mingle with editors, agents, publishers, and other writers.

Often, large workshops will host at least one session on publishing, and even if they do not, the people who are attending are likely to gab. The candid and insightful perspectives you're likely to overhear from this gabbing may even be more beneficial to you than any session could be.

You'll have a chance to learn about new and upcoming book genres. Readers' tastes are changing all the time, as are the technologies publishers are using to create and deliver books, and you want to stay on top of knowing what's out there, especially in terms of niche areas. The good thing about conferences and workshops is that you can meet the writers and editors of these new genres, and what could be better than learning about them from the experts?

Some writing conferences offer the opportunity to have your manuscript reviewed by professionals—editors, agents, and published writers. Occasionally you are given the opportunity to have face-to-face time with the reviewer of your manuscript, which is invaluable as a writer. It also gives you the chance to get your work to the decision-makers in the field. It can be very difficult to get your manuscript in the hands of an editor or agent, and many publishing houses will not accept unagented or unsolicited submissions, so attending the conferences is one of the only ways to make sure that your work gets read by the right people. You may also get the chance to learn things such as time management and story techniques from the best, and to discuss writing with those established authors you're striving to be like.

Going to a writer's conference, though, can seem a big and intimidating step. (There may also be an entrance fee, though your college or program may help you pay for it.) If you're not quite ready for that, talk to your faculty and ask them to recommend writers living nearby, especially ones who may have come to speak in your classes or given readings on campus. Your faculty may well be on first-name terms with them and will be happy to pass you along for a chat. This may seem pushy, but never forget that every writer was just starting out once, and they'll know all too well what you're up against.

Claire Bennet

Talk to people about what you want to do. People, especially older ones, love to help young people who are just starting out, and they love to hear about your plans. You would not believe how many connections in the writing world I've made just by telling people that I want to be a writer. Networking is hugely useful, and it never hurts to know more about the writing world. Be proud of what you do, and let others know about it!

Freelance

Here's the harsh truth: almost no one graduates from college with a full-time writing job. Like most things in life worth having, gaining that full-time spot at the *New York Times*, or wherever you want to end up, takes time and it takes a lot of building up your resume. But what you can graduate with is about a million opportunities at the tips of your toes. What I'm talking about is freelancing, and it's an underappreciated field that you should take advantage of.

The fact is, there are more writing opportunities out there than you ever considered, which means that you have more value than you realize. One of the worst things that you can do for yourself when you are first starting out is to undervalue the skills that you've acquired while in school. Don't think that just because you've always shown an aptitude for screenwriting that you can't branch out and try something else. Don't think that because your brilliant novel hasn't sold to anyone, you should give up on becoming a writer and settle for your job at Kmart. Freelancing can help you extend your range of writing because you'll be jumping on opportunities that you haven't thought of before and finding out whether it's something that suits you or not.

Probably the most important and beneficial thing to you is what you will learn about the business of writing. I bet you don't know much about the current rates for freelance writing. (Someone asks you to rewrite their website. How much should you charge?) You will. You'll also learn all about contracts, why you sign a contract, and maybe even what to do if the other end doesn't hold up to what they're signing to. You'll learn about copyright and liability as well. These are the things that are important for you to know, that will put you ahead of the competition right out of the gate if you understand them, and they are also the things that you didn't learn in the classroom. You have to get out there and experience these things to understand how the business really works.

Freelancing will help you to develop your personality. You'll have to become more outgoing if you're going to succeed. The jobs won't come to you, so you'll need to take initiative to go out there and find them, and then convince the person who put out the ad that you are exactly the person they are looking for. This will help you build connections, but also develop a thicker skin. As a freelancer, you are in many respects your own boss, and you have to make sure that you are paid accordingly to the work and effort that you're putting into the project, and are treated with respect by the person you are doing the writing for.

There are also benefits that go along with these new obligations. Much of the time, you are probably going to be working from your home or in your own space, so you can dress however you feel like dressing that day. It's only on the occasions when you have to meet with your client in person (if you do) that you have to act like a grown-up and dress professionally, depending on the client. You can also set your own schedule. If you want to sleep until two o'clock in the afternoon and stay up until the crack of dawn, you can do that because there's no one to stop you—as long as you get the job done.

As I've already said, there are many, many different types of freelance opportunities and freelance jobs. I won't try to list them all because there isn't enough time or paper in the world for that, but here are a few.

* **Web content writing.** There are a lot of Web content opportunities, some of which are very sketchy, some of which pay very badly. Pick your target carefully. It may be easier to pick up a job from Craigslist that offers a few dollars an article than it is to go out and make your own work, but you'd do much better in the long run to find websites that are badly in need of revision and pitch your services to the company. You'll face rejection some of the time, but not only will you earn more in the long run, you will get repeat work and referrals. And if you work for the website of a company or non-profit whose mission you like and believe in, you may be able to make a sideways move into a more permanent position.

* **Real estate writing.** Seriously. Any profession that has pamphlets or catalogues needs writers.

* **Alumni magazines.** Always looking for stories about undergrads or alumni doing interesting things—and they pay well.

* **Ghost writing.** An individual pays you to write an article/essay/book for them and their name goes on it. Hint: retirement homes are full of people who have stories to tell, and some will pay you to write their story for them.

* **Specialty blogs.** A huge opportunity for anyone who has an area of expertise: wine, rock climbing, snowboarding, fashion, specialty beers. Look for a company doing business in your area of expertise and offer to blog for them.

* **Musician/band bios.** If you are a college senior and you don't have friends in a band who badly need your writing skills, you've misspent your college years. From bios you move on to liner notes, then on-the-road blogs....

* **Journalism.** If you have some basic journalism skills and a streak of curiosity, you'll find a plethora of neighborhood papers that are somehow surviving the crash of the big presses. They may or may not pay you at first, but they'll be grateful and encouraging, and there's no better way to find out what opportunities lurk in your community.

When you're first starting out, it will be the biggest benefit to you if you become acquainted with a local freelancer (or five) and talk to them about the rates that they charge. Sometimes a project will warrant an hourly rate, and sometimes you will get paid a flat rate for the entire project (maybe half upfront and half at the completion of the project), so it's also important to find out what different rates you should charge for different projects. Make sure you get a really clear description of the project before you come up with your quote. No one expects an on-the-spot quote, so tell your client that you're going to take 24 hours to come up with a number.

Of course, you can always turn to the Internet to find out what rates are considered acceptable, but be wary of the region in which people making those rates are located. Depending on where you locate yourself post-graduation, you may be making more or less money than someone else doing the same job, but location is another important factor to take into consideration when coming up with your quote.

Range is important: you want to be careful of asking for an amount that's too low, as you don't want the client to think that you're unprofessional or amateurish. You also don't want to start out asking for the same amount of money that someone who's been in the field for 25 years is getting. It's all about a balancing act, so make sure you carry a scale wherever you go.

Above all, don't let all the facts and figures freak you out. You're just starting out, so of course you don't know all the ins and outs of the business yet. Just do your best to prepare yourself before you go face the wolves. Be eager, be resourceful, be resilient.

Krysta Voskowsky

Say yes to everything. Regardless of the genre in which you categorize yourself, if someone offers you the opportunity to earn money by writing or simply to write for free to put a credit on your resume, take it. When you think you can't write something, you're wrong. You can, and you will. Whether your approached with writing technical manuals, greeting cards, food reviews, or political propaganda, every single writing experience you have will teach you something and open doors to the writing projects you really desire, even if you don't know yet that you desire them.

Be professional

Potential employers have a curious, ready-to-jump-one-way-or-the-other attitude toward students.

On the one hand, they're all too ready to believe the worst of every student they meet, and the slightest sign of unprofessional conduct or self-presentation confirms their worst fears: you are indeed the lazy, illiterate, scruffy layabout they were afraid you were.

On the other hand, they would love to believe you are the great hope for the country's future, the sweet, hard-working, intelligent kid who will come into their business and shine with all the promise of youth.

Your job, then, is to tip the scale in your own favor. Here's how you do it.

* Make up your resume. Career Services can and will help. Make it clean, strong, well-laid-out, and individual.

* Have your own business cards made up. Seriously.

* Make sure your website is up to date.

* Buy a set of interview clothes.

* Create a portfolio of writing that spans the range of the writing you'd like to be paid to do, looks attractive on the page and is completely, utterly free of typos and technical writing errors. Have a printed version and an electronic version.

* Rehearse what you're going to say before you pick up the phone.

* Arrive on time for interviews and appointments. In other words, leave more time than you think you'll need, and get there early.

* Thank people for seeing you or talking to you. This may be the most important of all.

Alli Arbuthnot

Before you go into an interview, be sure you know why you want the job. You may have your pitch polished, but if you can't articulate why you want the job (other than a paycheck, that is), chances are you don't really want it that much at all. Not only will it show to your interviewer, but you may want to consider continuing your job search until you find something that lights you up inside.

Don't limit yourself

Think about your non-writing specialties. Whether you are great at social media or cooking or really active at living a green lifestyle, everyone has skills outside of the standard forms of writing. Make a list of those skills, and start brainstorming how you can use them to advance your writing career in outside-of-the-box ways.

> *One of the worst things that you can do for yourself when you are first starting out is to undervalue the skills that you've acquired while in school.*

Tommy Ngan

It wasn't until I developed my skills as a cook and learned to apply my new-found abilities that I realized how much I had to offer.

Here, the most important point I want to make is about something I wish I had done. I've spent most of my final semester listening to everyone else talk about the skills they have (such as the ones I've listed) and how they want to use those skills in new and interesting ways, and I wish I had taken the time to think about my own skills. Now graduation is right around the corner and I keep thinking, "Well, I'm insanely organized. So what can I do with that?"

The other day I was talking to my mother about graduation and my life plans, and I started to think about what I was good at. I'm organized. I'm obsessed with checking my email. I'm (generally speaking) on top of my shit. I love, and really excel at, research. I don't give up on things. Suddenly, being someone's assistant seemed like the perfect idea to me, and would involve writing in a way I never really gave much thought to before. But does that seem too ambitious? Of course not. That's how you climb the social ladder and networks. No one starts out as a CEO of a company.

I only wish I had started considering my strengths sooner. Then maybe I'd have a post-grad job lined up already.

Ian Frisch

Do not underestimate the power of entrepreneurship. The writing industry is heavily affected by the evolution of technology: The printing press is being dominated by Internet-based publication methods and information is more accessible by the general public, and therefore more easily generated. Because of this, aspiring writers are in prime form to make an impact on their own. In our heyday, writers were required to adhere to a publication and work their way up the ladder, being granted permission to meet the right people, whereas now-a-days, any journalist in their early 20s can pay $35 a month for Internet service and make a name for themselves. Moreover, if you can create an online presence that transcends into a real-life representation, such as a consistent event, you are gold.

Don't think your dreams are too small just because no one else is dreaming the same thing.

Emily Cummings

By now, you've come to realize that being a professional writer means more than publishing content for your readers. For one thing, "content" has shifted dramatically to include virtually all types of media. The methods used to publish have shifted too. And, that incessant debate, print vs. digital, continues.

After four years of college and many valuable conversations with professionals in the industry, I know that to be a professional writer I must be able to do more than write.

Never was this lesson more clear to me than this final year of college as I prepared to enter the workforce. While there are absolutely jobs that mainly consist of using your writing and editing skills, most employers today are looking for someone who has versatility within communications.

I applied for a job with a small press as a marketing director. The job description mainly asked that the individual be someone who "isn't afraid to work independently and who has strong publishing skills." However, after speaking with the employer on the phone about my application, it became quickly evident that she really wanted someone who was "young and eager to jump into online."

Luckily for me, I've already seen this trend coming and have begun learning Web development. The lesson here is, don't limit yourself skill-wise. You are capable of a lot; great communication skills are just one part of that. Find out what other unique skills you can harness and offer to future employers or clients. In the end, because of my unique skill-set for a writer I got the job. Look at industry trends, see what's being demanded, find your unique skills, build them, and you will too.

Imagine your own patchwork

Right now you're probably freaking out just a little and thinking, "I need to get a job. I need to get a job. I need to get a job."

It's likely that almost everyone in your year is thinking the same thing, but things are a bit different for a writer.

For one thing, if you look in the job ads you see positions for software engineers and financial analysts and speech therapists but not many for writers. That's not exactly reassuring.

For another thing, the whole idea of looking for That One Job brings up all kinds of questions. Maybe you like writing fiction, but you're also getting interested in screenwriting. Does that mean you have to choose between the two? And what if your favorite kind of writing is a genre (such as poetry) that just won't pay the bills, at least until you're famous? Does that mean you have to get a job you don't like in order to support your poetry?

I have some good news for you, or maybe just a different way of looking at the issue. The fact is, for better or worse, most writers don't have just one job. Most writers patch together a life from a surprising variety of pieces, and now would be a good time to start thinking about some of the patches in your life after graduation.

Courtney Weitz

The thought of constantly having multiple jobs excites me and scares me all at the same time. I love being busy. I thrive on it to an extent that is scary. I knew when I chose to be a writing major that life wouldn't be simple and that bills would be hard to pay, and life wouldn't be a breeze. Yet, even though I've always known that life would be hard, sitting here thinking about it scares the shit out of me. What if someday there comes a time when I can't handle a hectic life like I have now? What if things are even harder than I already expect them to be? A patchwork of jobs may seem great, but it is also terrifying.

Now I'd be the first person to admit that letting go of the idea of getting one job that takes care of all the bills is pretty scary, especially right after you graduate and those student loans start to come due. Before you run off and curl up in a dark corner with your favorite blanket, though, think of the pressure the Patchwork Method takes off you. It means, for example, that you don't have to commit yourself to love and cherish That One Job when maybe you don't even know if it's right for you. Think of it as casually dating a couple of jobs.

And chances are, it's hard to picture every little square in your patchwork plan right away. Things seem more frightening when they're unclear or hard to see, so let's try to imagine what some of those pieces might look like.

First of all, you haven't wasted the last three and a half years of your life. So what skills do you have? Once you stop thinking that you have to choose between those skills and instead think about how you can add them up, the picture starts getting clearer and less gloomy.

Mike Garris

I don't get bored at all while doing copyediting, and if I were to be getting paid well for doing it, all the better. Because copy editing can be the bread and butter of a freelance writer's income, I consider it a very good thing that I am willing to spend a good deal of my time doing copy editing.

Furthermore, my reviews seem to be pretty well received by those who read them. In general, I am a game reviewer, and writing game reviews is a passion of mine. I think it's because I spend so much time reading game reviews and playing games, but for some reason, when writing game reviews I just know what players really want to hear about in terms of what the game offers, and where it stumbles. It's a very niche skill to have, but it's still a skill, and if I could learn the ins and outs of any other form of entertainment, like theater or literature, and be able to write reviews for those as well, I could be in a good place to make even more freelance money.

Okay, so you have writing skills—and seeing as we're living in an age when those skills seem to be getting in short supply, those are good skills to have. What's more, the ability to write well is a skill you'll always have, and if you're like most writers, you may develop new areas of writing skill.

This leads me to the next point. You're a writer, but you're not only a writer. What interests do you have, in addition to writing, that might make your life feel interesting and worthwhile?

Sarah Frazier

I would also like to explore interests alongside my writing. Broad enough I know, but music, animal rescues, and science oriented things are a general interest I do have. I have this weird side dream of working at an orangutan rescue shelter as some sort of adventure-driven side job. I also decided a long time ago that my major plan B would be to start an almond farm in California and blog about it. Random, yes, but, random enough to be interesting.

Courtney Triola

Last year for spring break I went to Virginia and worked with Habitat for Humanity. The way I felt after spending a week doing that doesn't compare to anything else I've ever felt, and I want to keep having that feeling for the rest of my life. I'd love to become a long-term volunteer with Habitat. I know that Habitat offers grant writing positions as well, so there's another option that could also incorporate writing.

You don't need to think of yourself as a writer who must get a writing job based on the courses you've taken in college. If you are an Accounting major, you might have taken a bunch of courses in a particular area of accounting, and as a result you'll be looking for a job in that area. That's not how most writers develop their career. Most writers try all kinds of things, following a path that meanders all over the place, and often discover their own niche almost by accident. And they keep learning and picking up skills along the way. There's no map; it's the journey that matters.

So with that in mind, what patches are important to you even if they have nothing to do with writing? What will keep you sane and healthy? What will help you carry on being an interesting person, and therefore an interesting writer?

Sarah Lucia

I love writing but there are so many other things I want to do too. I work at a state park every summer answering phones and mowing lawns, and I love it. I love talking to the elderly couples who stay at our park for the peace and quiet, and I love being surrounded by the sun all day long.

I want to travel. There are so many places I want to go, and not just for a week. I want to go to places and spend a month, maybe two, who knows, maybe a year. I want to go to the Japanese countryside and spend weeks in the mountains surrounded by temples and amazing gardens. I want to learn to build my own bookcase. I want to design my own quirky style house with lots of windows and large open rooms and natural wood floors and walls. I want to live in a city. I want to live out in the middle of nowhere. I want to live in Maine. I want to live in Montana. And most of all, I want to publish novels.

Going back to the problem of the art that doesn't pay (yet), some of the patches may be writing activities that don't have an immediate financial payoff but are essential if you want to work towards being the kind of writer you want to be. Writing fiction is a good example: your fiction may well not pay anything immediately, but you need to keep working on it in order to improve to the point where it actually will pay off. It may seem as though you have to choose between starving in a basement while you work on your novel, or selling out and doing something you hate just to pay the bills, but there are plenty of other choices.

Jeff Nettleton

I grew up surrounded by farmers, lumberjacks, and construction workers. These are the sorts of jobs that I did for years before I came to college, and they're the jobs that will always be available to me later in life. I don't think I'll ever have trouble staying afloat, so long as I remain unafraid to get my hands dirty. I'll keep writing short stories and working on novels, even if I'm not getting paid for it immediately. Supporting myself off of this sort of work alone will be a goal that I strive for.

When you think about your life this way, it makes you start to realize that someone in another major, who may find it easier to get a full-time job straight away, may not even have stopped to ask what they want their life to be about, and what makes them feel a sense of purpose and satisfaction.

Pulitzer or Bust

You, on the other hand, are forced to think right away about these big questions, and thinking in terms of a life made up of pieces may mean you're more aware of what really matters to you. And at the same time you're developing the skills that one day may start pulling the separate pieces together into a job that combines several of your skills, and several of your interests.

Isn't that a bit less scary? And maybe even a little appealing?

Mike Garris

So with my current skill set, as well as the ones I am developing now, I would say that I have a firm platform to make some money post graduation. Even if I end up going into full time retail work with freelance writing on the side, that is a situation I could live with. I am really just happy that I now have some idea what I want to do with my degree post graduation. At any rate, it beats where I was six months ago, with no freaking clue.

Fifth Year

Of course, the time you really need friendly advice is right after you've graduated, when you leave behind almost everything you've known and start out in that scary and confusing thing called the real world. So we asked several recent writing graduates to think over the past one, two, three or even four years and give the advice they think will be most helpful to you as you make that transition.

Ginger Vieira

Don't waste the last six months of college thinking, "Free at last! I can just cruise through the rest of this!" The last six months is your opportunity to take everything you've learned so far and put it to use in a more professional stage. Find a internship that means something to you instead of getting one just to fill the course requirements so you can graduate. In the end, you might intern for a company you thought you'd really love, doing work you thought you'd love and find out that it's not actually a good fit for you. That's great to know! If you want to be a writer, dedicate yourself to creating great work during those last six months you can learn from and benefit from and use in your portfolio in the future.

Figure out what you really want to be doing with yourself at this point in your life and do it. If it isn't writing, that's okay, but if writing fits into there somewhere, go after that. There is a silly presumption about the writing world that you can't make money there...but how many times a day do you come across a website or a magazine full of words? You could find a job in there!

There are dozens of internship possibilities and website writing gigs that could lead to real jobs. MediaBistro.com is an example of a great website with continuous posts from magazines, newspapers, and online publications who are looking for interns. You could be one of the writers for those websites. You just have to guts to research, find the contact info and show them what you're worth.

In the end, do what you love most. If you want something to happen, don't spend all your time waiting tables while hoping for a miracle writing job to appear in your lap...go get that job for yourself.

> Ginger Vieira has lived with Type 1 diabetes and Celiac disease since 1999. In 2009 and 2010, Ginger set 15 records in drug-free powerlifting with personal best lifts including a 308 lb. deadlift, 190 lb. bench press, and 265 lb. squat. Today she is a cognitive diabetes coach at Living-in-Progress.com, personal trainer, author, and freelance writer and video blogger. She is the Mental Skills Coach for TeamWILD.org, and a diabetes health coach at DiabetesDaily.com. Find her YouTube Channel for diabetes video blogs at YouTube.com/user/GingerVieira.

Krysta Voskowsky

Learn as much as you can about managing your finances, then practice what you learn. A lot of people assume that because we are writers, we are not "math people." However true this statement may be for you, it does not exempt you from having (or parting with) money. Developing good financial habits early will set you up to be a successful professional writer for the rest of your life. Start saving for retirement in your early 20s and if you can swing it, keep an emergency fund that will cover eight months of living expenses. Balance your checkbook and stick to a budget, no matter how small. Live beneath your means. As writers, we aren't always guaranteed huge salaries off the bat, but the more you get a steady hold on managing your money, the less you will stress. The less stress you have, the more good writing will flow from you.

Be nice. Friendliness, sharing, politeness, and good manners will take you everywhere—but this does not mean becoming a doormat. You can be confident, aggressive and driven in your career goals while still staying graceful and personable. Honestly earn a reputation for being someone who's wonderful to work with as well as a great writer. If your mother never taught you, take the time to learn proper table manners. When traveling within another culture, have the wherewithal to research local traditions, customs, and social guidelines before you go and treat your hosts with utmost respect and gratitude. You kindness will walk you through doors you never thought possible. You will be a character magnet; people will open up to you when you least expect it. Not to mention, living a life of overall positivity can keep you calm, strong, internally healthy, and externally glowing.

> Krysta Voskowsky is working toward her MFA in Creative Non-Fiction at Lesley University.

David Karalis

When you're starting off freelancing, don't be too picky with your assignments. You need to get started, and sometimes the connection you make for a writing assignment you're less than thrilled about can lead to something much better.

Get organized and stay on deadline. A great way to lose work and burn bridges is to be flaky and be late on deadlines. Buy an organizer, or if you have a smartphone, integrate your Google Calendar with it (and actually keep your Google Calendar up-to-date).

When taking an assignment, don't be afraid to ask questions. People actually prefer if you ask these questions in the beginning of an assignment so they don't have to go back and correct it after the fact. This also shows you're serious about creating the best work possible.

Be as flexible as possible. Sometimes there have to be layers of feedback, and you need to write within the voice of a particular company or protocol. You need to sometimes just roll with it and be as accommodating as possible; this will make you easier to work with and potentially lead to more lucrative work.

Be patient. Drawing from my own experience, sometimes it takes a different path and a couple years of experience to finally grow into a more writing focused role. You might need to find a good company or reach a certain level within a company to uncover the writing opportunity a job/ career path poses. There are writing opportunities hiding around a lot of different corners.

Embrace your education. You went to college for writing. Never forget the things that you were taught. Just because information is easily accessible and easily generated by any person with an Internet connection does not mean that everything you read or see on the Internet is credible. The thing that will make you stand out to the right people—your press contacts, artists, and other, more established journalists—will be how well you write, and your professionalism in the public eye. Being a grammar Nazi, structure psycho, photo Fascist, and overall obsessive-compulsive journalist and editor will be more work for you, but will grant you shinier rewards in the end. And you'll get the one thing that people in this industry strive for the most: respect.

Be determined. Opportunities to get published and make a name for yourself abound. You just have to have an ear and eye to find them. Do your own research. Continue to learn. Read. Just because your college education is over doesn't mean that you have left the classroom. That's the beauty of journalism: You are always learning. If you are into a specific topic at that time—say music—read the music section of the New York Times and New Yorker every day. And studying specific publications that you may want to pitch articles to will give you the know-how in what ways to write for these people. But determination shouldn't stop at just trying to get published. There are many other rocks to pick up and uncover potential opportunities.

Leave town. Sorry, but you will not become a substantial writer in the same town as where you went to college. It's too comfortable, and, sooner or later, the pillow that you call Burlington will turn to quicksand and you'll be stuck there. Shake the president's hand, snag that piece of paper you've busted your ass for, get in your car and leave. Try someplace metropolitan and random. Try New York. Los Angeles. Chicago. Anywhere. Be stimulated at all times, and create opportunities for yourself by diving into the new and unknown. And, over time, you'll find out that the writing and journalism circles in these areas are smaller than you think, and a fresh, ambitious writer with talent and determination and a willingness to learn will not be easy to overlook.

Take risks. Don't be afraid to start your own thing, try out new niches that you may become passionate enough to write about, develop career OCD, give yourself high standards, move to a random place, only rely on yourself, be a trend setter, be aggressive, cold call once a week, wake up an hour earlier than normal, stay out an hour later than normal, switch up your coffee shop, go see bands you've never heard off, eat at a new restaurant once a week, stop smoking, shake up your life, and always write. Never stop writing.

> David Karalis is working for SEER Interactive, an Internet Marketing Agency in Philadelphia, PA. He is reponsible for growing a network of freelancers and creating content with them for a variety of different clients.

Jacquelene Adam

If you do not have a job lined up post graduation, do not freak out. A lot of people choose to travel or move home to save money, and some have no idea what they want to do. That is okay.

Don't be afraid to work for free. Intern for free, write for free, and work for free. Right now, any experience you can get, whether paid or unpaid, is essential. You will learn later that the work you did for free will pay off eventually.

Intern. Yes, again. Whether you did not get to while in school, or you still need to make more connections, I cannot stress enough that this is the best way to your career. After I graduated, I moved home and told everyone I knew or met what I wanted to do. I wanted to work for a magazine in New York City. Eventually after telling hundreds of people my story, I made a connection that landed me an internship at *Elle* magazine. It was unpaid and I had to work two other jobs just to pay the bills, but I was getting unbelievable experience at a top fashion magazine. While there I learned that fashion wasn't the industry for me and I wanted to pursue my dream of working at a travel magazine. I bounced around for a while at a few different jobs and eventually took an internship at *Conde Nast Traveler*. This was also unpaid. I am just now finishing the internship and my hard work is paying off. I recently interviewed for the assistant editor position at the magazine and have a few more interviews lined up at top magazines in NYC. I thought my dream of being a travel editor would never be and now it is right in front of me. Don't forget to dream big, work hard and be persistent. Your dream job will not come to you, you have to go out and find anyway possible to get it. Good luck!

Dream big. If there is a magazine, a publishing house or a newspaper that you would love to work for, apply for an internship there. Whatever it is you want to do, no matter how out of reach it may seem, it is usually closer than you think.

After spending two years with the travel writing industry in New York City, Jackie Adam now works for an event production company and blogs for the Somaly Mam Foundation, a non-profit dedicated to protecting women and children from slavery. She has also started her own company called CARRY, which sells tote bags to benefit various charities.

Claire Bennet

Do what you need to do. Things are tough for everyone right now. I had to move back in with my parents (as did most of my graduating class), and that was hard for me to do, because I felt like I should be taking my degree and going out to forge an autonomous existence for myself from day one. But the times are such that often you have little choice. It's not writing advice, but I think it's also important, because you'll likely be dealing with a lot of worry and anxiety and depression after graduation, and that's normal. Don't do anything because you think it's what you're "supposed to do." Do what you need to do. You'll be a lot happier if you live life on your own terms.

All of life is an experience, and everything you do becomes fodder for your own writing. Now is the time of our lives when we have the freedom to go off and do cool things. I just spent three months down in North Carolina at a folk school, which exists to bring the craft and culture of Appalachia to the general public. I gardened, and mulched, and split wood, and greeted students, and weeded, and cleaned. It was a lot of tough work, and it was one of the best experiences of my life. If you're between jobs and having trouble getting another, don't sweat it. Look for other cool things to do. You have the rest of your life to anchor yourself into corporate America (or find ways not to). For now, take advantage of your freedom to go and experience the world, and you'll be a better writer for it.

Never give up. If you have stories to share with people, never stop looking for ways to share them. Every little victory counts for something. Think about how different things would be if J.K. Rowling had thought, "I'll never be accepted" and thrown out the napkin that was the beginning of *Harry Potter*. Imagine if J.R.R. Tolkien had convinced himself that people weren't interested in fantasy, or if Stephen King had decided there were already too many people out there writing horror novels. Never be afraid to visualize yourself being successful. Before you can convince other people that you can make it, you have to convince yourself.

Pulitzer or Bust

Never stop writing. It sounds obvious, but it's absolutely key. Write every day. Write because it's what you love to do. The only difference between authors and wannabes is that the authors are the ones who sat down and actually did the writing. I don't need to tell you how wonderful writing is, because if you're in this major, you already know. Just make sure to repeatedly remind yourself why you love it.

Be persistent—and don't ignore your mother's advice. I currently work as a bookseller on the children's floor of the Northshire Bookstore in Bennington, VT. It's a really neat place, locally run, and is well known for its great atmosphere and unique approach to bookselling. My mom happened to see an ad on their website for the position, and e-mailed it to me. I applied right away and heard nothing. A few days later, we heard from a friend that the owner of the store said they were not hiring. I was pretty bummed because I was excited about the job, but because of a cool internship I'd just had, I knew that the head of an organization doesn't always know what's going on down on the lower tiers. I called, and e-mailed, and went personally into the store until they gave me an interview. When I was offered the job, my boss thanked me for my persistence. So I can tell you first hand that it really, really pays to not give up at the first sign of rejection. Keep going until you get a definite answer. I'm now working an amazing job that gives me a really solid understanding of the market in which I some day hope to publish, because I proved to my boss that it mattered to me. You'll probably hear a lot of "Don't get your hopes up," but don't take it to heart.

Claire Bennet is currently working in quality assurance for Turbine, Inc., a video game company that publishes *The Lord of the Rings Online* and *Dungeons & Dragons Online*. She is wrestling with the manuscripts for several Young Adult fiction novels while ambitiously (and perhaps naively) planning out her next big steps in life.

Eric Voorhis

Once you graduate it will be very easy to stop writing. Don't do it. Force yourself to write at all costs, even if you don't land a job in the field.

Finding a job is a job in itself. After a few odd jobs after college I began working for a small newspaper in upstate New York. It never would have happened if I didn't make writing cover letters and sending resumes a big part of my life for a month or two. It might seem like a daunting task to get a job writing, but it's not. There are plenty of jobs out there; you just have to work hard at it.

Strange jobs are okay. I had a great experience working for a newspaper as a general assignment reporter, but I did miss the strange jobs I had prior—which were both better paying. Despite what your parents may think, there's nothing wrong with working in a restaurant, bar or cafe, after college. I'm sitting in a public library in Billings, Montana, my new home as of last Friday. Just got back from three days of backcountry training and first aid classes at a small camp just north of Missoula, and I'm about to start a seven-month-long season as a crew member of the Montana Conservation Corps. Next Monday I'm leaving for a 21-day trip with six other crew members to cut new trails in the Shoshone National Forest, which covers a big chunk of Northwestern Wyoming. I'm looking forward to a few months of trail work, swinging an ax, wielding a chainsaw and generally trying to be a badass while living out-of-doors for long periods of time. Plus, nothing gets me thinking like some good manual labor. It's a little strange to trade in a steady job and a salary for volunteer work and a modest stipend, but I couldn't be more thrilled. On the other hand...

...You're trained to write. We're in the age of the Internet, which means citizen journalism and endless blogs. But you're trained to write. You have valuable and marketable skills that most people don't. Take yourself and your work seriously.

Eric Voorhis is a journalist and photographer living in Road Town, Tortola—capital of the British Virgin Islands—where he covers courts and writes features for the *BVI Beacon*. A former staff writer for the *Lake Placid News* and *Adirondack Daily Enterprise*, he is a native of Long Island. During his time at Champlain College he wrote about scuba diving, yaks and paranormal investigators.

Devin Beliveau

Have a dedicated workspace. I've tried doing work on my bed, in my living room while roommates watch TV, at the break room at work... It never works out. A desk and good work chair is key. If I had a proper desk in my room I would get a lot more work done. Which brings me to my next tip...

Practice time management. I don't have a consistent schedule, so I can't dedicate the same time each day, but I schedule myself a day in advance. I try to give myself two hours a day to either read or write, depending on what I'm working on at the time.

Read, read, read. And read things you might not usually read. Two of my recent favorite books were ones I bought just based on their covers and they turned out to be amazing. I'm also a big fan of Amazon.com and I often buy books based on their suggestions (in the used section of course, for about $2.50 per book). Reading good books always renews my love of writing and makes me want to write immediately after I finish a book.

Keep a journal or blog. Whether it's personal or private, keeping a journal or blog is important. If I have an idea, I need to write it down immediately or I will usually lose sight of it. I keep a whole personal website to remind me of the goals I have.

Look into writing workshops or author presentations where you live. I moved to Boston after graduating, and there are always presentations from authors at various venues, and usually for free or for a very small fee. Just like reading constantly, these events always make me want to write as soon as I get home.

Devin Beliveau is enjoying life in Boston working for Apple and hanging out with friends as much as she can. She daydreams about planning perfect vacations while reading her favorite travel and photography blogs. And she (of course) jots down ideas in the Five Star notebook she carries around, with the hope that one day it will all come together.

Alli Arbuthnot

Learn how credit works. No credit is bad credit; if you don't have a credit card, get one. Establishing good credit is crucial these days, and in some big cities you can't even rent an apartment if you don't carry plastic. On the flip side, if you have a credit card (or several), for the love of God, keep it under control. Now is not the time to bury yourself in debt, especially if that debt is dirty martinis and Urban Outfitters. It's not worth it! Let me say that again: It's not worth it!

Cultivate your confidence, but turn in your pride with your cap and gown. This, my friends, is not an easy world that you're walking into. If you find yourself waiting tables in six months or a year (or more), don't get down on yourself! Seriously. It's an honorable and character-building thing to work odd jobs as a means to an end. Keep your chin up and don't quit pursuing your goals. You know what you're worth. Something will come along.

Don't compromise on your dreams—but do allow room for evolution. With time and experience, your vision of your dream job may change. While you should hold fast to your goals, don't keep them so close that you can't or won't see other opportunities opening up around you. Life is full of surprises, and they are beautiful. Good luck!

Allison Arbuthnot currently lives on the beach in Los Angeles, CA, with her cat Rocky and fiancé Tom. She is the Associate Editor of Cooking.com, and continues to work as a freelance food and health writer and recipe developer.

photo credit: Trish Tomlins